B   Sanderlin, George   5487
Gama

         Eastward to India

                    Date Due

EASTWARD TO INDIA
Vasco da Gama's Voyage

EASTWARD TO INDIA

Vasco da Gama's Voyage

by George Sanderlin

Illustrated by Alan E. Cober

Harper & Row, Publishers   New York

GRATEFUL ACKNOWLEDGMENT IS MADE FOR PERMISSION TO REPRINT
SELECTIONS FROM THE FOLLOWING BOOKS:

The Lusiads of Luiz de Camões. Translated by Leonard Bacon. Courtesy
of The Hispanic Society of America.
St. Francis Xavier (1506–1552) by James Brodrick, S. J. Copyright
1952 by Pellegrini & Cudahy. Reprinted by permission of Farrar, Straus
and Giroux, Inc.; Burns & Oates, London.

Selections from the following books are reprinted by permission of the
Hakluyt Society, London:
The Chronicle of the Discovery and Conquest of Guinea by Azurara.
Translated and edited by C. R. Beazley and E. Prestage.
The Voyages of Cadamosto. Translated and edited by G. R. Crone.
The Three Voyages of Vasco da Gama by Corrêa. Translated and edited
by Hon. H. E. J. Stanley.
The Prester John of the Indies by Alvarez. Translated by Lord Stanley.
Edited by C. F. Beckingham and G. W. B. Huntingford.
Esmeraldo de Situ Orbis by Pereira. Translated and edited by G. H. T.
Kimble.
Travels by Varthema. Translated by J. W. Jones. Edited by G. P. Badger.
The Voyage of Pedro Alvares Cabral to Brazil and India. Translated and
edited by W. B. Greenlee.
A Journal of the First Voyage of Vasco da Gama, 1497–1499. Translated
and edited by E. G. Ravenstein.

EASTWARD TO INDIA
Text copyright © 1965 by George Sanderlin
Illustrations copyright © 1965 by Alan E. Cober
Library of Congress Catalog Card Number: 65-20247

To Frea, Mary, David, and Johnny

Contents

Maps and Illustrations

Author's Note

Most of this book consists of selections from early Portuguese or Italian histories, logbooks, books of travel, etc., as translated into English for the Hakluyt Society. Omission of some of the words of the original source within a sentence is indicated by three dots; omission of a sentence or more from the source is indicated by four dots. In a few places, sentences of the original source are transposed so that the order of events will be clearer.

The spelling of place names is modernized (e.g., "Calicut" for "Calcoen"), and names of persons are usually given in the forms adopted by Boies Penrose in his *Travel and Discovery in the Renaissance.*

Words inserted by a translator to make his meaning clear and enclosed by him in brackets are not bracketed here. Words inserted by the present editor for additional information (e.g., "Don Lourenço" after "our captain") are bracketed. Words inserted by the present editor in place of a word or phrase of the original source are bracketed. Punctuation and capitalization of the sources are, for the most part, retained, but the paragraphing is the present editor's.

G. S.

Introduction

Heeled over under the wind, a small ship—a caravel sent exploring by Prince Henry of Portugal—moves slowly down the west coast of Africa. Each of its three triangular sails is painted with the great red cross of the Order of the Knights of Christ.

"Good is that which passeth," chants the cabin boy as he turns the sandglass. "Better that which cometh."

"Port your helm!" shouts the pilot to the steersman.

"Ah, I hope this wooden nag brings us home safe to Lisbon," a seaman mutters.

Some of the crew of thirty are busy scrubbing the deck. Others sleep, rolled in blankets amidships, untroubled by the flying spray. On the quarterdeck the commander, a nobleman, stares at the distant shoreline.

The caravel is far from port, farther south than Europeans have ever sailed. Sometimes at night, after the entire company has chanted the Latin hymn to the Blessed Virgin Mary, the *Salve Regina,* the sailors frighten each other with tales about this "Green Sea of Darkness" they are voyaging over, the Atlantic Ocean.

"The Bishop of the Seas—" whispers one, and breaks off while his comrades imagine the dread bishop of legend with his phosphorescent miter.

"Or the Sea Unicorn—" adds another, with a shiver. The Sea Unicorn has a horn which can transfix three ships at once!

Nevertheless, the Portuguese caravel sails on, into the unknown. Propelled by the ancient faith of the crusaders and by the new desire to learn, it is sailing right out of the

Middle Ages into an era of discovery and progress for western Europe.

In the short space of a hundred years (1420–1520), the exploits of the Portuguese mariners were to dissipate the gloom which overhung Europe during the fifteenth century. Their discoveries would extend through half the globe and lead to Columbus's voyage to America. And little Portugal, poverty-stricken and unheeded on the outskirts of Europe, would establish the first world empire, a fantastic collection of islands and fortresses stretching from Morocco to China.

Newfoundland, Formosa, New Guinea, Brazil, and the Cape of Good Hope are half a world and more from Lisbon, but all were found and named by the Portuguese.

What led to this splendid achievement? How did it happen that while France and England were struggling through civil wars, only slowly becoming aware of lands beyond the Mediterranean, Portugal was knocking at the gates of China? Or that the first European to sail around Africa (Vasco da Gama) and the first man to circumnavigate the globe (Ferdinand Magellan) were both Portuguese?

We may seek answers to these questions by looking at the land and its people, at the ships in which the Portuguese sailed, and at the leaders who planned and carried through their expeditions.

The Land and Its People

In a passage in the *Odyssey*, Homer speaks of a land "at the ends of the earth, where life is easiest. No snow is there, nor great storm, nor ever any rain; but always Oceanus sends forth the breezes of clear-blowing Zephyrus." Some scholars think this land was Portugal, and Spain.

Portugal is a coastal strip on the west of the Spanish peninsula, a nation created by its own heroic history rather than by geography. That is, no wall of mountains partitions Portugal from Spain; no great river or desert borders and isolates it. Geography seems to have intended this country to be part of Spain, but its inhabitants were drawn together by their struggle against the Moors on the Atlantic seaboard into a sturdy little kingdom too proud to merge with the rest of the peninsula.

So Portugal, shaped like a shoebox stood on end, and about the size of Maine or Indiana, claimed its separate place in the family of Christian nations. It measures only 362 miles at its greatest (north-to-south) length, 140 miles at its maximum (east-to-west) width.

In the north, Portugal is mountainous and rainy. In the south, the Algarve is a province of brilliant sunshine, of oranges, lemons, and olives—the orchard of the nation—with white, flat-roofed villages as in North Africa. Because it borders the Atlantic, Portugal is cooler and more fertile than Spain. Most of the country consists of rolling hills, of moorlands covered with flowers, of farms and small fishing villages along the sandy coast.

Although Portugal did not become an independent nation until the twelfth century, its people even then had a rich past from which they could draw inspiration. For example, the love of adventure which stirred in Vasco da Gama and other explorers may be an echo of Phoenicians and Greeks who sailed to Portugal in their trading ships. The ancient name of Lisbon, capital of Portugal, was Olisipo, fancied to be derived from the name of the city's legendary founder, Ulysses.

Perhaps Portuguese endurance and willingness to work hard are a legacy from the disciplined Roman legions of Augustus. Rome drove the Carthaginians from Portugal in 201 B.C. and called the country *Lusitania*, after its natives. Portuguese law is based on Roman law, and the name "Portugal" itself comes from the Roman name for the important Portuguese city of Oporto: *Portus Cale* ("Warm Port").

After six centuries of Roman rule, Portugal and Spain, like the rest of the Empire, were overrun by barbarians (A.D. 409–418). A Visigothic (West Gothic) kingdom was founded on the Spanish peninsula, which endured until A.D. 711.

Moslem Arabs conquered Spain and Portugal (A.D. 711–715), and governed unchallenged for over three hundred years. Christians called these invaders "Moors." Unquestionably the Portuguese of the age of discovery owed much of their knowledge of mathematics and geography to scholars trained in Arab schools. The Arabs preserved the works of Greek scientists, such as Aristotle and Ptolemy, and transmitted them to Europe during the later Middle Ages.

In the eleventh century, at long last, Christian princes in the mountainous north of the Spanish peninsula sallied forth to fling their defiant battle cry, "*Santiago!*" against the ringing "*Mahomet!*" of the Moors. (*Mahomet* is a form of "Mohammed.") Crusading knights from all over Europe rode to help the kings of Leon and Castile. St. James (Santiago), patron of Spain, was reported mounted on a white charger in the skies, leading the Christians against the Moors with a flaming sword—and in the wake of the Arab retreat the nation of Portugal was born.

One of the crusading knights who helped the king of Leon was Henry of Burgundy. In recompense for his services, the king of Leon bestowed upon Henry, in A.D. 1095, one of his less desirable daughters and also one of his less desirable tracts of land, the remote "County of Portugal." In 1147 the son of Henry of Burgundy recaptured Lisbon from the Moors. This was a great victory, secured with the aid of the "fighting monks" of the Middle Ages, the Knights Templars and Hospitallers, who were passing through Portugal on their way to attack the Infidel in Palestine.

Religious-military orders appealed to the rugged Portuguese. They founded four such orders, including, in 1319, the Knights of Christ, whose members served on many exploring expeditions and supplied the religious fervor which helped carry the Portuguese to the ends of the earth. About this time the Portuguese navy was also begun.

When the Spanish kings decided that Portugal should be brought under their rule, they discovered they had waited too long. Although greatly outnumbered, the Portuguese routed the forces of Castile at the battle of Aljubarrota (1385) and confirmed their independence. Then they made a lasting alliance with England (English archers fought beside the Portuguese at Aljubarrota), the oldest alliance in the world today. Philippa, daughter of John of Gaunt, of England, married Portugal's King John I and became the mother of Prince Henry the Navigator, who inaugurated the age of discovery.

The Portuguese of Prince Henry's fifteenth century, *fidalgos* and commoners alike, were proud men. (*Fidalgo* means "son of somebody," i.e., of gentle birth.) They were not very tall, but were muscular and durable, brown-skinned and black-haired. Their features, as though softened by the ocean breezes, were more rounded than those of the aquiline Spaniards.

They were both practical and poetic. On voyages to Africa, India, or Brazil the Portuguese sailor would stolidly suffer from scurvy or risk death in battle, but was also quick to break into a smile or join Hottentots or South American Indians in a gay dance. He called his compass "the rose of the winds." He would scrupulously name each new land for the saint on whose feast day it was sighted, and just as piously cheat primitive peoples by exchanging beads, ribbons, or other trash for their gold.

"May the Devil take thee! What brought you hither?" a dweller of India asked the first Portuguese ashore from Vasco da Gama's fleet.

"We came seeking Christians and spices," was the reply, combining the deep religious feeling of the Portuguese with their hardheaded interest in profits.

As long as the courage and faith of the Portuguese people redeemed their cruelty and intolerance of other creeds, they succeeded in the mission which destiny gave them. Their caravels anchored in waters undreamed of by the Greeks and Romans. The medieval banner of Portugal, with its five shields (*quinas*), was unfurled on coasts inhabited by African bushmen and jeweled Eastern sultans; and the reports of Portuguese voyages, eagerly read in Europe, cast a bright light into the future.

Ships, Astrolabes, and Compasses

Although fifteenth century Portugal, with only a million inhabitants, was not overcrowded, it was a poor country. It lacked what Americans would call a frontier; the hinterland, the "back country" toward Spain, was undesirable, and there was not much of it. When the Portuguese realized there were fortunes to be made overseas, they rushed to enlist. Soon a good proportion of the young men were to be found on the Atlantic and Indian oceans.

In what kinds of ships did they sail? How did they find their way across the wilderness of the Ocean Sea—the Atlantic and other oceans thought of as surrounding the inhabited earth?

The earliest type of Portuguese ship was the *barca:* a small, clumsy vessel with just one mast, carrying a square sail. But their chief model, the one which became their trademark, was the graceful caravel.

The caravel was developed from a fishing boat, a craft similar to that seen today in Lisbon Harbor with a wide-open eye painted on either side of the prow so the boat may find its way through the Atlantic fogs. Long, light, and relatively low in the water, the caravel had a flat stern and a sharply curved bow. It was from 65 to 100 feet long and 20 to 25 feet wide. Can you imagine fifty men living for months packed in a space about equal to that of a tennis court?

The caravel carried three "lateen" (triangular) sails, which enabled it to tack, that is, to sail against the wind at an angle, a maneuver especially useful on the return voyage from Africa. "Lateen" comes from the word "Latin" and refers to the use of the triangular sail in the Mediterranean.

Each sail was slung to a pole with tapering ends, and the pole was attached to a stumpy mast at about a 45-degree angle, like a railroad semaphore pointing downward. Later in the fifteenth century the Portuguese favored the *caravela redonda*, which had square sails on the foremast and mainmast and a lateen sail only at the stern, as steadier for ocean voyaging. (Columbus's beloved *Niña* was a *caravela redonda*.)

The caravel was of shallow draught so it could slide over sand bars and poke into rivers when exploring strange coasts. At the rear a high "castle" rose, containing the captain's and officers' quarters; in front was the "forecastle," a storeroom where the sailors sought shelter during storms. Magellan's men clung together in such a forecastle, weeping and praying in a hurricane until the star-shaped discharges of electricity known as "St. Elmo's fire" glowed on the masthead and were taken as a sign that the storm was passing.

The sailors stowed their belongings in lockers lashed to the open maindeck, in the waist of the ship. Below, there was the low-ceilinged gundeck (invented, with its ports for cannon, by a Portuguese king). The gundeck was not much more than a narrow ledge around the large hatch leading to the hold. The hold, occupied by trading goods and vermin, always had bilge water sloshing around its bottom.

Another ship used by the Portuguese was the *nao*, a cumbersome vessel with square sails. It was also called a "round ship" because its length was only three times its width. Vasco da Gama's flagship was a *nao*, a type which, because of its greater width and deeper draught, provided added safety. Very large *naos* used as storeships were often destroyed before the end of a voyage, when enough supplies had been consumed so that the remainder could be transferred to other ships.

A ship's size was measured in the number of "tuns," or casks of wine, it could carry. *Barcas* were always under 100 tons. Caravels were usually listed at 50 to 200 tons; *naos* were often over 400 tons. To give the sizes in modern ship's tons, you would have to increase the fifteenth century figures by about one-sixth.

Once King John II of Portugal ordered some storeships broken up after they reached the Guinea coast of Africa simply because he was spreading a rumor that "round ships" could not sail back to Europe against the prevailing winds and currents. He wanted other maritime powers to believe that only the caravel, a type monopolized by the Portuguese, could make this voyage.

"I can bring *any* ship back from Africa, I don't care how big it is!" one of John II's pilots argued at the king's dinner table.

"A stupid fellow thinks he can do anything!" snapped the king, and changed the subject.

Later, in private, John II apologized to his pilot, explaining that he knew what the pilot said was true, but that he didn't want to reveal any secrets to competitors. Indeed, the Portuguese pursued such a strict policy of secrecy in their African voyages, because of the profits involved, that in 1504 King Manuel I decreed the death penalty for anyone giving out unauthorized information.

The Portuguese explorers worked their way down the unknown African coast by carefully noting each headland, river mouth, or, even, grove of trees, like Mark Twain learning to pilot on the Mississippi. They made portolan (sailing directory) charts of this coast. But when they ventured west into the "Green Sea of Darkness," the Atlantic, all landmarks disappeared over the horizon and they had to trust to compass, astrolabe, and seaman's intuition.

A pilot guides his ship across the oceans by locating his position in relation to lines of latitude and longitude, an invisible grid or "street plan" of the globe first drawn up by the Greek geographer Ptolemy. The Portuguese, like all their contemporaries, were baffled by longitude but could determine latitude.

Thus a Portuguese captain always knew with rough accuracy the direction of his voyage, and how far north or south of the equator he was, but he could not do much more than guess at his east-west position. His compass gave him his direction and his astrolabe his latitude, but the chronometer (accurate ship's clock) which would enable him to fix his longitude was not invented until the eighteenth century.

Neither did he have a log line by which to measure his rate of speed. For an educated guess, he tossed an object overboard at the prow of the ship (or he spat!) and timed its drift to the stern with a sandglass. Caravels averaged six or seven miles an hour.

What, exactly, is latitude? The "parallels" of latitude may be compared to cross streets in a city. They run horizontally around the world and are numbered beginning with the equator, the parallel around the middle of the world, as 0°. A navigator voyaging "up" from the Congo to Lisbon would count how many parallels, or degrees, he had crossed north of the equator. He would reach Lisbon at almost 39° "north latitude," that is, almost 39° north of the equator. The North Pole, which is at a right angle to any spot on the equator, lies at 90° north latitude; the South Pole lies at 90° south latitude.

The "meridians" of longitude are the avenues, which run vertically from the North Pole at the top of the world to the South Pole at the bottom. A Portuguese captain sailing west into the Atlantic and discovering Brazil could try to figure how many meridians, or degrees, of longitude he had crossed, counting from the "prime meridian" (0°), which in the fifteenth century was drawn through the Canary Islands. He would measure his longtitude "east" or "west" of the prime meridian. All the way around the world, a complete circle, would be 360°.

Since a navigator could not measure longitude accurately, he usually practiced "parallel sailing": he went north or south to the desired latitude, then turned east or west and followed that line of latitude, like a freeway, to his destination.

A simple way to determine latitude, as long as the caravels sailed above the equator, was to measure the height of the North Star, in degrees, above the horizon. This height, in degrees, *is* the latitude of the observer. At the equator, for example, the North Star disappears—is just under the horizon—so the latitude is 0°.

The Portuguese often measured the height of the North Star with the astrolabe: a disk with a pointer, like a clock with one hand. The astrolabe was graduated in degrees; between "nine o'clock" and "twelve o'clock," for example, would be 0° to 90°. One man held the astrolabe suspended by a thumb ring at its top, another aimed the pointer at the North Star, and a third read off the angle which the pointer made with the "horizon line" (from "nine o'clock" to "three o'clock") on the disk. Sometimes the Portuguese used a quadrant or the T-shaped cross-staff.

Whatever the instrument, the pitching of the ship made sighting a star or the sun, at sea, extremely difficult. It was like trying to hit a clay duck in a shooting gallery with the floor tilting under your feet. Whenever possible, the Portuguese took their observations on land.

Below the equator, where the North Star is invisible, the Portuguese could compute their latitude by measuring the height, in degrees, of the sun above the horizon at noon if they also had a table giving some technical data about the position of the sun in relation to the celestial horizon. Two famous Jewish mathematicians, Abraham Zacuto and Joseph Vizinho, around 1482, provided the mariners with just such tables of the declination of the sun.

For direction the Portuguese depended upon the compass, probably invented by Italian navigators or scientists and known in Europe since the twelfth century. It consisted of a magnetized needle fastened so as to swing freely above a card mounted in a round bowl. The needle pointed roughly north, but "declined" slightly toward northeast or northwest in different parts of the earth because the geographical and magnetic poles do not coincide. Columbus was one of the first to note this "variation of the compass."

On the compass card, north was marked by the petal-shaped fleur-de-lis (as it still is today). The other points were not indicated by letters or numbers, as now, but by markings of different shapes, lengths, and colors, radiating from the center of the card—because many of the sailors were too illiterate to read letters and numbers.

Although Portugal produced the most skilled seamen in Europe, the commanders of some later expeditions ran short of experienced men. One captain found that his sailors could not grasp the terms "starboard" (right side of the ship) and "port" (left side), so he hung a bunch of garlic over his caravel's right gunwale and a bunch of onions over the left, then barked his commands in language the ex-farmers could understand:

"Garlic your helm!" (Steer to the right!)

"Onion your helm!" (Steer to the left!)

Guided by the compass in its hooded box which was illumined by a tiny lamp, charted by sightings of sun or North Star made with big wooden or smaller brass astrolabes, adorned at the prow with a carved figure of the saint the ship was named after, the rakish, three-masted caravels and round *naos* plunged into the unknown.

The Search for Spices

What were the Portuguese seeking?

They were hoping to find the mysterious Christian ruler, Prester John, about whom more will be said later, and they also sought to strike a blow against the Moors of Africa and Asia. But in addition to these idealistic goals, the Portuguese had a very practical one. They were sailing thousands of miles to obtain what we casually pass each other at the dinner table: pepper.

Pepper and other spices were the oil and uranium of the fifteenth century, the sources of wealth and power. Pepper was literally worth its weight in gold, and was often used as money. Europe's demand for the spices of the East seemed insatiable.

One explanation of the vast demand is that spices were used for perfumes, medicines, and as items in the manufacturing process (e.g., as bleaches, dyes, etc.). But the chief reasons that importers of spices became millionaires—called "pepperbags" by the Portuguese—were the monotonous diet of western Europe and the absence of refrigerators.

Through the long, snowy winters the people yearned for seasoning to make their black bread, oatmeal, and smoked meat more appetizing. They especially needed pungent condiments for the meat, which began to spoil soon after the fall slaughterings; they would pay exorbitant prices for good strong pepper that would overpower the odors of decay. (Europe lacked fodder to keep cattle alive until spring—hence the annual fall slaughter.)

The coat of arms of the rich Fugger merchants of Germany showed a camel bearing a bale of spices. The Fuggers bought spices on the bustling Rialto of Venice, the chief market of Europe, and shipped them north to be distributed by traders of the Hanseatic League. The Venetians acquired them from the Egyptians, who had received them from caravans traveling to Cairo from the Red Sea.

Portugal's aim was to substitute a caravel for the camel. The Portuguese hoped to carry the spices from India around Africa to Europe—in Portuguese ships. At one stroke they would deprive Arab traders in the Indian Ocean, Arab and Egyptian caravans by the Red Sea, and Venetian galleys in the Mediterranean of their business. Since a handful of dried berries, nuts, roots, leaves, and pieces of bark picked up off the ground in Indonesia for a few pennies increased ten thousand per cent in price by the time they reached London, the profits at stake were enormous.

The Portuguese had their first windfall on the Guinea coast of Africa. A Negro chief offered them some red grains of what looked like dots of cake icing. When the seamen tasted it, they grimaced and rushed for the water cask. Their mouths felt hot enough to propel the ship! The "icing" was melegueta pepper. The first cargo delivered in Lisbon created a sensation (and several fortunes). After Europeans became used to the taste, they called the peppercorns "Grains of Paradise."

Black pepper grew wild on the slopes of the Western Ghats, behind Calicut, India, but the real spice factory of the world was a handful of islands with "fiery hills" (volcanoes) in Indonesia. Indonesia itself is a curving trail of three thousand islands flung out into the Pacific beyond Singapore. The Molucca, or Spice, Islands, lie on the equator in the midst of this archipelago.

In addition to pepper, which is the fruit of a plant, the desired spices included another fruit (nutmeg), a root (ginger), bark (cinnamon), and a spike-shaped bud (cloves—from French *clou*, meaning "nail"). At this time cloves were the most valuable of all spices, and were found only in the Moluccas; they grow in crimson clusters at the ends of the branches of a tall, beautiful evergreen. Gums, resins, and narcotics, found in India and Arabia, were also classed as spices.

Merchants transporting spices from Indonesia to Europe ran many risks. Sailing from the Moluccas, they passed between islands infested with Chinese pirate junks and might have their cargoes stolen—and their throats cut with a wavy-edged *kris*—long before they reached Calicut, in India. In Calicut merchants had to pay a huge tariff to the Indian ruler (the Zamorin) and transship their goods for the voyage to Suez, at the head of the Red Sea.

More pirates lurked off the Indian coast. Then, after the spices were transferred to camel caravans at Suez for the trek to Cairo, at two miles an hour, Bedouin robbers awaited them in the desert, ready to whirl out of gullies or from behind ridges for plunder. On the voyage from Alexandria to Venice the Turkish navy tried to blockade the ships, while Salee pirates, who would auction off captives in the slave markets of Tripoli, hunted them.

But the high profits justified taking the risks. Indeed, after Vasco da Gama reached India, other European nations envied Portugal and sought new routes to the East for themselves. Since Popes Nicholas V and Calixtus III, in 1454 and 1456, had granted Portugal a monopoly of exploration to the south, Spain was willing to consider Columbus's plan to seek a westward passage. Twenty-nine years after Columbus's voyage, Magellan's men, also sailing in the service of Spain, reached the Moluccas by the westward route and continued around the world. But by that time the Portuguese were too well established in the East to be driven out.

Take a good look at the pepper shaker on the dining room table at your next meal. It helped inspire Columbus to discover America!

Pioneers of the Sea

Portuguese *fidalgos* and commoners, the "sons of somebody" and the fisherman-farmer "sons of nobody," crowded together on the small caravels in quest of spices. Prince Henry the Navigator, King John II, and the nobleman Vasco da Gama played the chief roles, but captains of the middle or lower classes also won lasting fame.

The Portuguese voyages actually represented a "second front" for Christendom in its struggle with Islam. In the fifteenth century Islam was expanding, Christendom shrinking. After 1291 every wave of crusaders, with their crosses of silk or gold stuff sewn on their tunics, had fallen short of Jerusalem. Christian kings gave only lukewarm support to new crusades preached by the popes, and the papacy itself was stained with corruption.

Worst of all was the relentless onward march of the Ottoman Turks. These fierce nomads, who had been driven from central Asia to Asia Minor by the Mongol invasions of the Middle Ages, captured Constantinople, the great barrier-city that protected Europe, in 1453. By the end of the fifteenth century the Turks would overrun Greece and the Balkans, and devastate Poland. Early in the sixteenth century their armies would take Budapest and ring Vienna itself with hundreds of white tents and siege machines.

This Moslem threat to Europe was just developing when, in 1415, the Portuguese made an unexpected sally across the Strait of Gibraltar and stormed the Moroccan city of Ceuta.

One of the victors in that attack was a black-haired giant with the deep-set eyes of a dreamer but the firm mouth of a man of action: Prince Henry the Navigator. Prince Henry was a Grand Master of the Knights of Christ who fasted and wore a hair shirt most of his life, but whose "answers were always gentle." It was in Ceuta that Henry had the idea of organizing expeditions to sail south along the coast of Africa. These expeditions would seek "knowledge . . . of the Indies, and of the land of Prester John."

(Prester John, whose realm is described on p. 59, was supposed to be a Christian king descended from one of the Three Wise Men, dwelling somewhere in the East. He was both priest and king—*prester* means "priest"—and fabulously wealthy. Unfortunately for the Portuguese, he was also legendary; there was no Christian king in Asia. "Prester John" finally came to be used merely as a title for the king of Ethiopia, who was Christian.)

On Cape St. Vincent, a windswept promontory at the extreme southwest of Portugal, where Europe ends, Prince Henry established a base, the "Naval Arsenal." Beyond the rocky cape stretched the unexplored Ocean Sea, in which, according to an ancient Greek writer, the sun set "with a noise of sizzling." But in Prince Henry's day the only "sizzling" came from the activity of his shipbuilders, captains, mathematicians, astronomers, and mapmakers.

Here the Portuguese built their first caravels. They sailed fifty-one of them south in thirty years, rediscovered the Atlantic islands, mapped and charted fifteen hundred miles of hitherto unknown shoreline, and by the time of Henry's death, in 1460, reached the rich Guinea coast, with its ivory, slaves, and gold.

For twenty years after Prince Henry's death, exploration lagged, until, in 1481, a youthful ruler of boundless energy, patience, wisdom, and decisiveness came to the throne: King John II, the "Perfect Prince." King John was determined to solve the problem of the southern half of Africa and the sea route to India.

Ancient and medieval geographers thought of the world as consisting of a hemisphere of land (Europe, Asia, Africa) bordered by an encircling Ocean Sea which covered the other (western) hemisphere. But they had only vague notions of the far east and the far south of the land hemisphere. Ptolemy, for example, taught that Africa was connected to an antarctic continent, and that the Indian Ocean was a landlocked sea which could not be entered from the Atlantic. He imagined you could walk from the bottom of Africa east and then north to China. Other geographers drew Africa as an island which did not extend far south; they thought you could sail east along the coast of Guinea straight to India.

Europeans in the fifteenth century were even uncertain about the exact location of India. Under the term "The Three Indias" they sometimes included the African territory of Ethiopia.

In 1487 King John called upon Bartholomew Dias, an experienced captain and outstanding navigator, for one of the greatest of Portuguese voyages, a voyage which would disprove Ptolemy's theory and open the way for Portuguese conquest of the East. Dias sailed with three ships under orders to round Africa, if possible, *and he succeeded!* He wanted desperately to go on to India, but his crews, frightened by the uncharted seas, refused. He is the discoverer of the Cape of Good Hope.

John II suppressed all news of Dias's achievement because he feared competitors would use the newly discovered sea road. But on the docks the king talked excitedly to Dias about Dias's ideas for altering the design of caravels so they could better withstand the storms off the Cape of Good Hope. And in his council chamber King John pondered an intelligence report from his agent, the veteran traveler Pero de Covilhan, who had journeyed overland to India, then south to Sofala, on the east coast of Africa, where he confirmed Dias's finding that there *was* a sea route around that continent.

Then on March 4, 1493, a tempest-battered ship arrived at Lisbon with unexpected and chilling news. Its tall, blue-eyed Genoese commander, now sailing for Spain, announced with supreme confidence, "I have just returned from Asia, which I reached, as I said I would, by sailing west."

The Genoese was Christopher Columbus, with several long-haired, dark-skinned captives, back from the discovery of America.

Panic swept the Portuguese capital. King John's committee of scholars still could scarcely believe that Columbus had found Asia, only 2,400 miles west of Europe, as he had proposed to do nine years before when they rejected his project. But when King Ferdinand and Queen Isabella of Spain followed up Columbus's success by persuading their countryman, Pope Alexander VI, to grant them broad rights south and west in the Ocean Sea, rights which threatened the Portuguese monopoly in Africa, King John II prepared for war against Spain.

Spain yielded, and in 1494 signed the Treaty of Tordesillas. This treaty divided the whole world into two halves, by a meridian drawn from the North Pole to the South Pole at 46° 30′ longitude west of Greenwich. Spain agreed that Portugal would have exclusive rights to trade

and to claim new lands in the eastern half, which included Brazil, all of Africa and India, the Malay Peninsula, and the Spice Islands. Spain would have similar exclusive rights in the western half.

The Treaty of Tordesillas was a triumph for Portugal. It was followed, four years later, by the supreme moment in the history of Portuguese exploration, and perhaps in the history of Portugal itself.

King John II had died, and Manuel the Fortunate now reigned. King Manuel, a lanky, athletic man with a talent for choosing outstanding commanders (and also for treating them ungenerously), had just sent Vasco da Gama with four ships on his famous voyage to India.

It was May 20, 1498. The thickset da Gama, with his black spade beard and weathered, brick-red features, his square jaw thrust forward, peered across a stretch of water at a strange shore behind which rose steep mountains crowned with heavy rain clouds. Da Gama's Arab pilot pushed back his turban and pointed.

"That is the country which you desired to go to," he said.

The mountains were the Western Ghats. The Portuguese had reached India.

Immediately the Arab traders in the area reacted with furious hostility. They urged the Zamorin of Calicut to oppose the intruders. Two years later fighting broke out in Calicut and war flamed across the Indian Ocean.

The Portuguese had two great advantages which helped them win the war: caravels and cannon. We have already viewed their long, light vessels which could sail into the wind or easily run away from any Arab trader afloat. The Portuguese superiority in artillery was still more marked. Gunpowder had been introduced into Europe in the fourteenth century. By the end of the fifteenth century, gun carriages had become lighter and had been placed on wheels, iron projectiles had replaced stones, and the Portuguese even contrived "powder-pot" hand grenades for close fighting. They fired their cannon from the newly invented gundeck, through portholes.

In contrast, as late as 1502 there were only two cannon to defend the entire city of Calicut. Their gunners made no attempt to aim the pieces, but used them like giant firecrackers, relying on the "Bang!" of the discharge to frighten away the enemy.

Because of these advantages, a force of nineteen Portuguese ships commanded by gallant Francisco de Almeida routed an Egyptian-Indian fleet of over one hundred vessels in the crucial battle of the war. This battle, one of the decisive conflicts in world history, was fought off Diu, in northwest India, February 2, 1509. At the end of the day, Portugal ruled unchallenged in the seas from the Cape of Good Hope to Ceylon.

The sequel to Almeida's victory was the Portuguese overseas dominion, which expanded to include the Spice Islands and the island of Macao, just off the mainland of China. From bases in East Africa and along the Malabar Coast of India, where they made Goa their capital, the Portuguese monopolized the commerce of the Indian Ocean. Gold, silver, precious gems, spices, tapestries—luxuries all but unknown in Europe since the fall of Rome—poured into Lisbon.

A twentieth century traveler glimpses the traces of past elegance in the impressive white limestone Abbey of the Jeronimos, which King Manuel built to commemorate Vasco da Gama's voyage. Here, on the site of the humble chapel where da Gama prayed before setting sail, rises a monastery reminiscent of an Indian temple.

In it are tombs supported on the backs of black marble elephants, and shaded cloisters in which the decorative motifs of the pillars are spheres, ropes, anchors, coral, and the cross of the Knights of Christ, all fantastically intermingled. This was the "Manueline" style of architecture of Portugal's day of glory.

Most of that far-flung empire has since been lost. After a century, parts of it were seized by the Dutch, then by the English, and now by the Afro-Asians. Brazil won its independence. Today Portuguese Guinea, Angola, Mozambique, and a few islands are the only territories left, and how long they will continue under Portuguese control is uncertain.

But the Portuguese conquest of the sea and their discovery of half the globe remain one of the epics of mankind. Like Ulysses, who is said to have founded their city of Lisbon, the mariners of Portugal sailed into the unknown and added immeasurably to man's knowledge: of navigation, of the outlines of coasts to the south and east, of winds and currents of two oceans, of customs, peoples, and products of Africa and the Orient.

Their voyages marked the end of the Middle Ages, the beginning of the advance of Western civilization around the world.

From Prince Henry the Navigator's bare study at Cape St. Vincent, with its windows of delicate Moorish traceries open to the sound of surf, to the blue waters of the roadstead in which Vasco da Gama dropped anchor before Calicut, their story now unfolds.

EASTWARD TO INDIA
Vasco da Gama's Voyage

1
Prince Henry the Navigator

For he was the Discoverer of the Sea,
Who the Moor's swollen vanity put down
And entered first the gate of Ceuta town.

—Luis de Camoens, *The Lusiads*

The Victor of Ceuta

Prince Henry the Navigator was twenty-one years old when he took part in the Portuguese capture of Ceuta, in North Africa, in 1415. His father, King John I, had attacked this Moorish stronghold opposite Gibraltar to provide an occasion for knighting Henry and two other sons.

Henry is described by a biographer as "tall, broad-shouldered, long-limbed," with hair that was "thick, shaggy, and black." Although considerate of others, he had an iron will—which was about to find its goal.

When the Moors surrendered, Henry was sweaty with heat and dust and fighting. He removed his helmet, made his way to the center of the city, and stumbled upon his life work. As the third of the five sons of King John I and his English wife Philippa, Henry had little chance to succeed to the throne. But suddenly he knew what he did want to do.

He stood in the Moslem marketplace, where the merchants' booths had been overturned and their goods scattered. But what rich and exotic goods they were! Henry stared at the ivory elephants' tusks and red grains of melegueta pepper, the pale ostrich plumes, glittering salt crystals, dark gum, and shining yellow gold dust.

"Where do these goods come from?" he asked some Moorish prisoners, guarded by Portuguese crossbowmen.

"From the great desert," the Moors replied. "Some from the Gold Coast of Guinea."

Intently, Henry continued his questioning. Guinea, just above the equator in Africa, was fabulously wealthy. Henry wanted to know what routes the camel caravans followed, what cities they passed through, how long it took to travel from Guinea across the Sahara to the Mediterranean. And then he had an idea.

Why couldn't the Portuguese sail south, past the Sahara Desert, and trade directly with Guinea by sea? Perhaps they could find the half-legendary Christian king Prester John, or sail all the way to India!

Henry's deep-set eyes gleamed; his weariness left him. He was not the first to think of outflanking the Moslems, of going around their countries of North Africa, Egypt, Asia Minor, and Arabia to reach the East by sea and attack them from the rear—but he would be the first to act in a systematic way upon this idea. So the age of discovery may be said to have begun in Prince Henry's mind in captured Ceuta. He suddenly realized that the ocean was not a barrier but a highway.

Even though Henry himself never navigated beyond sight of land, he is called "the Navigator" because his work led to the voyages of Columbus, da Gama, and Magellan. The determination, idealism, courage, and courtesy of the Infant Henry ("Infant" means "son of the king") are well described by the historian Eannes de Azurara in the selection below.

Azurara wrote his *Chronicle of Guinea,* the source of our selection, in 1452–53 at Prince Henry's request. It tells the story of Prince Henry's African explorations.

[Prince Henry] was of a good height and stout frame, big and strong of limb, the hair of his head somewhat erect, with a color naturally fair, but which by constant toil and exposure had become dark. His expression at first sight inspired fear in those who did not know him, and when wroth, though such times were rare, his countenance was harsh. [When angry, Henry would wave the wrongdoer away, saying, "I commend you to God. May you be fortunate!"]

His bearing was calm and dignified, his speech and address gentle. . . . Strength of heart and keenness of mind were in him to a very excellent degree, and beyond comparison he was ambitious of achieving great and lofty deeds. . . . All his days were passed in the greatest toil . . . [and] it would be hard to tell how many nights he passed in which his eyes knew no sleep. . . .

[In the conquest of Ceuta] key of all the Mediterranean sea . . . the Prince was captain of a very great and powerful fleet, and like a brave knight fought and toiled in person on the day when it was taken from the Moors. . . .

Now the first Royal Captain who took possession by the walls of Ceuta was [Prince Henry], and his square banner [of St. Vincent] was the first that entered the gates of the city. . . . On that day the blows he dealt out were conspicuous beyond those of all other men, since for the space of five hours he never stopped fighting, and neither the heat, though it was very great, nor the amount of his toil were able to make him retire. . . .

For about two hours the Prince and his [four] friends held [a] gate . . . in a turn of the wall under the shadow of the castle. . . . And to this had retired the greater part of the Moors who had fled . . . but in the end, despite the great multitude of the enemy, they [the Prince and his companions] shut that gate. And whether their toil were idle or no could well be seen by those who had fallen and lay dead there, stretched out along that ground.

In that city of Ceuta was the Infant [Prince

Henry] knighted, together with his brothers, by his father's hand, with great honor, on the day of the consecration of the Cathedral Church. And the capture was on a Thursday, the 21st day of the month of August, in the year of Christ 1415.

Prince Henry's Dream

Not long after the capture of Ceuta, Prince Henry tossed and turned in his bed one night, unable to sleep because of his vivid memories of the African goods in the Moslem marketplace. At last he fell into a troubled sleep and dreamed.

Duarte Pacheco Pereira, a later Portuguese navigator, describes Prince Henry's dream in his *Esmeraldo de Situ Orbis (Guide to Cosmography)*, written around 1505–08. The historian Barros adds that when Henry woke he leapt up, shouted for his servants, and ordered ships prepared at once for a voyage south along the African coast.

One night, as the Prince [Henry] lay in bed, it was revealed to him that he would render a great service to Our Lord by the discovery of [Africa], and that in this region a great multitude of new peoples and black men would be found . . . whose color and shape and way of life none who had not seen them could believe; and that many of these peoples would be saved by the sacrament of Holy Baptism.

It was further revealed to him that in these lands so much gold and other rich merchandise would be found as would maintain the King and people . . .

of Portugal in plenty and would enable them to wage war on the enemies of our holy Catholic faith.

Five Reasons for Exploring Africa

Prince Henry was a man of the Middle Ages in his ardent religious faith, but a man of the Renaissance, just like Columbus, in his commercial and scientific interests. Both sides of Henry's nature are shown in the reasons he had for exploring Africa, as listed by Azurara in his *Chronicle of Guinea*.

After the taking of Ceuta [Prince Henry] always kept ships well armed against the Infidel [the Moors], both for war, and because he had also a wish to know the land that lay beyond the isles of Canary and that Cape called Bojador, for . . . up to his time, neither by writings, nor by the memory of man, was known with any certainty the nature of the land beyond that Cape. . . .

And because the said Lord Infant [Prince Henry] wished to know the truth of this . . . he sent out his own ships against those parts. . . . And this was the first reason of his action.

The second reason was that if there chanced to be in those lands some . . . Christians, or some havens, into which it would be possible to sail without peril, many kinds of merchandise might be brought to this realm . . . and also the products of this realm might be taken there, which traffic would bring great profit to our countrymen.

The third reason was that, as it was said that the power of the Moors in that land of Africa was very much greater than was commonly supposed . . . therefore the said Lord Infant exerted himself . . . to [learn] . . . how far the power of those infidels extended.

The fourth reason was [that] . . . he sought to know if there were in those parts any Christian princes, in whom the charity and the love of Christ was so ingrained that they would aid him against [the Moors].

The fifth reason was his great desire to make increase in the faith of our Lord Jesus Christ and to bring to him all the souls that should be saved . . . whom the said Lord Infant by his travail and spending would fain bring into the true path.

The Academy at Cape St. Vincent

Cape St. Vincent, in the southwest corner of Portugal, was the Cape Kennedy of the fifteenth century. It was a steep, rocky promontory, shaped like a ship and washed on three sides by the Atlantic Ocean. From this desolate headland the tenacious Prince Henry launched the expeditions which rolled back the curtain of darkness to the south—like King Arthur, one of Henry's boyhood heroes, sending out knights of the Round Table.

Prince Henry, who never married, devoted most of his life to exploration. He settled at Cape St. Vincent, perhaps as early as 1418, building a town enclosed like a naval base within one hundred acres and first known as the

"Naval Arsenal" but later called the "Villa of the Infant." It contained a palace, a church, a chapel, a study, an arsenal, a dockyard, a fort, and the first observatory ever built in Portugal.

Here Henry pored over documents brought him from Italy by his brother Pedro: maps and the writings of Marco Polo. Henry welcomed to Cape St. Vincent leading mapmakers and students of navigation, such as Master Jacome of Majorca. These scholars, many of them Arabs or Jews, made the charts, compasses, astrolabes, and tables of navigation for Prince Henry's captains. Around 1440 Henry's shipbuilders designed the first caravels here. His captains kept log books on their voyages and wrote down their observations of the African coast.

In Roman times Cape St. Vincent (now named for a Christian martyr) had been known as the "Sacred Promontory" (*Sacrum Promontorium*), because the gods were supposed to occupy it at night. So Prince Henry's town was also called Sagres (from *Sacrum*).

The selection below, describing the promontory, is from Azurara's *Chronicle of Guinea*.

That noble town which our Prince [Henry] caused them to build [is] on Cape St. Vincent, at the place where both seas meet, to wit the great Ocean sea and the Mediterranean sea. But of the perfections of that town it is not possible to speak here at large, because when this book was written there were only the walls standing, though of great strength, with a few houses—yet work was going on in it continually.

According to the common belief, the Infant [Prince Henry] purposed to make of it an especial mart town for merchants. And this was to the end that all ships that passed from the East to the West should be able to take their bearings and to get provisions and pilots there, as at Cadiz—which last is very far from being as good a port as this, for here ships can get shelter against every wind (except one that we in this Kingdom call the cross-wind), and in the same way they can go out with every wind, whenever the seaman willeth it.

Moreover, I have heard say that when this city was begun, the Genoese offered a great price for it; and they, as you know, are not men that spend their money without some certain hope of gain. And though some have called the said town by other names, I believe its proper one . . . was that of "the Infant's town," for he himself so named it.

Sagres, or "the Infant's town," was growing rapidly when Azurara wrote his *Chronicle*, in 1452–53. Nearby Lagos, the port of departure for many of Henry's expeditions, was crowded with strangers drawn by Prince Henry's reputation—Genoese, Venetians, Catalans, French, English, Germans, Arabs, Jews, Moors, Ethiopians, and even Indians. Europe, Africa, and the Orient met here.

The offer of Genoa to "buy" Sagres was really an attempt to secure a base—like the bases the United States has leased around the world, except that the Genoese wanted theirs for trading rather than defense purposes. They wanted a concession to build a factory (storehouse for trading goods) and establish a colony in the town.

Portugal did not believe in helping a competitor, however, and refused the offer.

The Atlantic Islands: The Madeiras

As we explore outer space today, we know the exact location of the planets we hope to reach and a good deal about the difficulties our astronauts face. Mariners persuaded by Prince Henry to sail for him, however, embarked upon a sea whose bounds were only guessed at, a sea containing no one knew how many islands, monsters, and marvels. For Europeans, as for Arabs, it was the much feared "Green Sea of Darkness."

Henry himself probably did not accept the estimate of one early geographer that there were 27,000 islands in the Atlantic. He had some knowledge of the three real island groups in the eastern Atlantic which his ships were likely to bump into: the Madeiras, 535 miles southwest of Lisbon; the Canaries, 340 miles south of the Madeiras; and the Azores, 830 miles west of Portugal. All were drawn, inaccurately, on medieval maps.

But Henry wanted to find out more about them. Between 1418 and 1432, before his ships had sailed much below Morocco, Henry took advantage of the accidental rediscovery of the Madeiras to have all three groups explored. He found that two of the groups, the Madeiras and the Azores, were uninhabited, and promptly began to colonize them.

These island groups had an ancient history, which Prince Henry may also have discovered in his midnight studies. The Greeks and Romans knew the Canary Islands as the "Fortunate Islands" (*Fortunatae Insulae*), and the Romans knew the Madeiras as the "Purple Islands" (*Purpurariae*). In the twelfth century the "Lisbon Wanderers," eight Moors from Lisbon, sailed to both the Madeiras and the Canaries, as perhaps did Vikings who coasted Africa, attacking the "Bluemen" (Moors). A Genoese captain rediscovered the Canaries in the thirteenth century, and in the fourteenth century two runaway English lovers (Robert Macham and Anne of Dorset) were driven by a storm to the Madeiras and died together there.

Prince Henry was more interested in science than romance. In 1416 he sent a ship to discover the cause of the strong ocean current between the Canary Islands, the first expedition of this type on record. Then in 1418 two daring young squires of his household, John Gonçalves Zarco and Tristão Vaz Teixeira, were blown to the Madeiras, and in 1420 Henry sent them back to plant a colony there.

Azurara narrates the adventures of the Madeira colonists below. The selection is from his *Chronicle of Guinea*.

Now it was so, that in the household of the Infant [Prince Henry] there were two noble esquires [John Zarco and Tristão Teixeira], brought up by that lord, men young in years and fit for great deeds. And after the Infant returned from raising the siege of Ceuta . . . these men begged him to put them in the way to perform some honorable deed. . . .

And the Infant, perceiving their good wills, bade them make ready a vessel in which they were to go on a warlike enterprise against the Moors, directing them to voyage in search of the land of Guinea, which he already had purposed to discover.

And since it pleased God to ordain such a benefit . . . He guided them so that, even with the weather against them, they reached the island that is now called Porto Santo, being nigh to the island of Madeira. . . . And so they remained there for some days and right well examined the land, and it seemed to them that it would be a very profitable thing to people it.

And returning thence to the Kingdom, they . . . described the goodness of the land and the desire they had as to its peopling; and this pleased the Infant much, and he straightway took order for them to obtain what was needful to enable them to return to the said island. And as they were . . . making ready for their departure, there joined himself to their company Bartholomew Perestrello, a nobleman . . . and these men . . . set out on their voyage to the said island.

And it happened that among the things they took with them to stock the said island was a she-rabbit, which had been given to Bartholomew Perestrello by a friend of his, and the rabbit went in a hutch pregnant, and it came about that it gave birth to young on the sea, and so they took all these to the island. And when they were lodged in their huts . . . they set free that female rabbit with her young to breed; and these in a very short time multiplied so much as to overspread the land, so that our men could sow nothing that was not destroyed by them. . . .

Wherefore they abandoned that island and passed over to the other isle of Madeira. . . . This second island they discovered to be good, especially in very noble flowing waters . . . [and] they saw that the land had good air and was healthy, and they found many birds, which in the beginning they were wont to capture in their hands. . . .

So they let the Infant know all this, and he straightway labored to send there other people . . . in the year . . . 1424.

Under Prince Henry the Madeiras prospered. The first children born there were named "Adam" and "Eve." Later in the century Columbus married a descendant of the same Perestrello whose rabbit caused so much trouble.

Another adventure of the first settlers, a terrible fire which threatened them, is described below by a later writer, Cadamosto. Cadamosto also tells about the products of the chief island, including fine cedar and yew woods and the malmsey grape, from which one of the famous wines called Madeira is made.

Cadamosto was a Venetian sea captain who sailed for

Prince Henry and wrote his *Voyages*—a selection from which is printed below—between 1455 and 1468.

[This island] is called the "Isle of Madeira," that is to say, the "island of timber," for, when first discovered by the men of the said Lord [Prince Henry], there was not a foot of ground that was not entirely covered with great trees [in Portuguese *madeira* means "wood"]. It was therefore first of all necessary, when it was desired to people it, to set fire to them, and for a long while this fire swept fiercely over the island.

So great was the first conflagration, that . . . this Zarco, who was then on the island, was forced, with all the men, women, and children, to flee its fury and to take refuge in the sea, where they remained, up to their necks in water, and without food or drink, for two days and two nights . . . to escape destruction. By this means they . . . cleared the ground for cultivation.

The Atlantic Islands: The Canaries and the Azores

In 1402 a French adventurer named Jean de Béthencourt made a partial conquest of the Canary Islands. He left his conquest under the governorship of his nephew who, in 1418, "sold" the Canary Islands to Prince Henry. In 1424 Henry sent a great expedition numbering 2,500 infantrymen and 120 cavalry to complete the conquest.

Unfortunately, de Béthencourt's nephew had also "sold" the Canary Islands—which were not legally his—to two other parties. Besides, fifty-eight years before de

Béthencourt arrived on the scene, Pope Clement VI had granted the Canaries to Spain.

Although the Portuguese tried to conquer the islands in 1424, 1446, and 1466, all three attempts failed. In 1479, by a treaty, Portugal accepted the Spanish claim to the Canary Islands.

The Canary Islands were so named by the Romans because they found many huge dogs there ("Canary" from Latin *canis*, meaning "dog").

Both Azurara and Cadamosto have left descriptions of the Canary Islanders and their primitive customs. The selection below is Cadamosto's later but more vivid account, from his *Voyages*.

The people of the four [Canary] islands subject to the Christians are Canarians. They speak various languages and can scarcely understand each other. There are no walled towns on the islands, only villages. They have not been subdued in the mountains. . . .

The other three [islands], inhabited by heathens, are larger, and much more densely populated, particularly two, Grand Canary, with about eight to nine thousand souls, and Teneriffe, the largest of the three, with about fifteen thousand souls. . . .

Of Teneriffe . . . it must further be mentioned that it is one of the highest islands in the world, and in clear weather can be seen from a great distance . . . for there is a point, or rather a mountain in the center of the island like a diamond which is very high and burns continuously. . . .

CORVO

FLORES

GRACIOSA

TERCEIRA

FAIAL

SÃO JORGE

PICO

AZORES

SÃO MIGUEL

SANTA MARIA

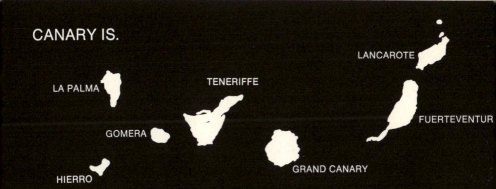

CANARY IS.

LANCAROTE

LA PALMA

TENERIFFE

FUERTEVENTUR

GOMERA

GRAND CANARY

HIERRO

In this island there are nine lords among them, called dukes: they are not rulers by natural law, where the son succeeds the father, but by right of the strongest. And they continually wage war among themselves, slaying each other like beasts. They have no other weapons than stones and sticks like spears, which are tipped with a sharpened horn in place of iron. Those which have no horns are sharpened at the tips, and the wood is made as hard as iron: and with these they attack. . . .

They have neither walled houses nor huts of straw, but live in caves or caverns in the mountains, sustaining themselves on barley, flesh and goats' milk of which they have plenty, and on fruits, particularly figs. . . .

They have no faith, nor do they believe in God: some worship the sun, others the moon and planets, and have strange idolatrous fantasies. . . .

These Canarians also are lightly built, great runners and jumpers, for they are accustomed to the crags of this most mountainous island. They leap from rock to rock, barefooted, like goats, and clear jumps of incredible width. They throw stones accurately and powerfully, so that they can hit whatever they wish. They have such strong arms that with a few blows they can shatter a shield in pieces. . . .

They always go naked, save some who wear goatskins, before and behind. . . . Both men and women paint their skins green, red, and yellow with pastes of herbs, and they consider that such colors are a beautiful device, esteeming them as we do fine clothes.

When the Portuguese reached the Azores, only 1,054 miles from Newfoundland, they were well on their way to America. It was in the Azores that Columbus saw a rock—which seemed to be a statue of a horseman pointing west—and took it as an omen for his voyage.

Prince Henry sent expeditions under Gonçalo Velho to explore the Azores in 1432, and to begin colonizing them in 1444–45. Flemings as well as Portuguese came, but Portugal retained control of these green garden islands, which the colonists called Azores (Portuguese *açor*, meaning "hawk") because of their numerous hawks and buzzards. Their first name had been "The Western Islands."

Since the Portuguese government adopted a policy of secrecy—not revealing all discoveries, not permitting new charts and maps to circulate—there may have been other western voyages we do not know about. Some Portuguese historians claim the Portuguese reached Brazil *before* Columbus discovered America.

Around 1447, according to the historian Galvão, certain Portuguese made a mysterious voyage. A ship was "carried westward by a storm . . . and arrived at an island where there were seven cities, and people who spoke our language." Returning to Portugal, the crew of this ship told Prince Henry that they had gone to church with the islanders and found sand which was one-third gold. But when Henry ordered them to sail back to this island, the ship disappeared.

Their "Island of the Seven Cities" was named Antillia, one of the legendary islands of the Atlantic. Antillia, located by mapmakers only 2,500 miles from Japan, was supposed to have been colonized by seven Christian bishops who, with their congregations, fled there from the Moors in Spain in the eighth century. Actually it did not exist; the crew's story is considered nothing but a tall tale.

Cape Not and Cape Bulge

The first Portuguese *barcas* sent south by Prince Henry crept timidly down the African coast for short distances, then quickly returned. The Portuguese rounded each cape fearfully, like a small child entering a darkened room at night. What would the seamen find lying in wait for them beyond that point of land? Above all, would they be able to sail back past the cape from the other side and get home safely?

Two capes were especially feared: Cape Non and Cape Bojador. Cape Non, translated into English, is "Cape Not." The Portuguese made up a rhyme about it:

> *He who passes Cape Not—*
> *Either he will return, or he will not!*

Actually "Non" is not derived from the Latin word for "not" (*non*) as the Portuguese thought, but from Arabic *nun*, meaning "fish." And the Portuguese did get past it and were able to return.

Cape Bojador, two hundred miles farther south, was a bigger obstacle. *Bojador* means "bulge." "Cape Bulge," below Morocco, not only marked the end of the known world for the fifteenth century but was swept by fierce currents which hindered navigation. It was low and sandy, hard to see from a distance, with an ugly, protruding reef that could rip the bottom out of a ship.

Whoever doubled this cape, the sailors whispered, would be carried into the terrifying region of the equator, where humans could not survive or, at the least, where white men would turn black. There the sea boiled, and the water ended in a hideous swamp filled with serpents.

Azurara, in his *Chronicle of Guinea*, tells of these fears and of how, in 1434, because of Prince Henry's insistence and in spite of fourteen previous failures, the Portuguese finally conquered Cape Bojador—and thus took the first step on the sea road to India.

So the Infant [Prince Henry], moved by these reasons, which you have already heard, began to make ready his ships and his people . . . but . . . there was not one who dared to pass that Cape of Bojador and learn about the land beyond it, as the Infant wished.

And to say the truth this was not from cowardice or want of good will, but from the novelty of the thing and the widespread and ancient rumor about this Cape. . . . How are we, men said, to pass the bounds that our fathers set up, or what profit can result to the Infant from the perdition of our souls as well as of our bodies—for of a truth by daring any further we shall become willful murderers of ourselves? . . .

For, said the mariners, this much is clear, that beyond this Cape there is no race of men nor place of inhabitants: nor is the land less sandy than the deserts of Libya . . . and the sea so shallow that a whole league from land it is only a fathom deep, while the currents are so terrible that no ship having once passed the Cape will ever be able to return. . . .

During twelve years the Infant continued steadily at this labor of his, ordering out his ships every year to those parts, not without great loss of revenue, and never finding any who dared to make that passage. . . .

At last, after twelve years, the Infant armed a *barca* and gave it to Gil Eannes, one of his squires. . . . And he [Eannes] followed the course that others had taken; but touched by the selfsame terror, he only went as far as the Canary Islands, where he took some captives and returned to the Kingdom.

Now this was in the year . . . 1433, and in the next year the Infant made ready the same vessel, and calling Gil Eannes apart, charged him earnestly to strain every nerve to pass that Cape, and even if he could do nothing else on that voyage, yet he should consider that to be enough.

"You cannot find," said the Infant, "a peril so great that the hope of reward will not be greater, and in truth I wonder much at the notion you have all taken on so uncertain a matter—for . . . you tell me only the opinions of four mariners, who come but from the Flanders trade or from some other ports that are very commonly sailed to, and know nothing of the needle [compass] or sailing chart.

"Go forth, then, and heed none of their words, but make your voyage straightway, inasmuch as with the grace of God you cannot but gain from this journey honor and profit."

The Infant was a man of very great authority, so that his admonitions, mild though they were, had much effect on the serious-minded. And so it appeared by the deed of this man [Eannes], for he, after these words, resolved not to return to the presence of his Lord without assured tidings of that for which he was sent.

And as he purposed, so he performed—for in that voyage he doubled the Cape, despising all danger, and found the lands beyond quite contrary to what he, like others, had expected.

2
Gold and Slaves

We must pray God for the soul of Prince Henry, for his discovery of this land [Sierra Leone] led to the discovery of . . . Guinea . . . and to the discovery of India, whose commerce brings us an abundance of wealth.

—Duarte Pacheco Pereira,
Esmeraldo de Situ Orbis (Guide to Cosmography)

The First Captives

After Gil Eannes had sailed past "Cape Bulge" a second time, in 1435, and, like Robinson Crusoe, had seen the footprints of men on the sandy shore, Prince Henry was eager to learn more about the inhabitants. A war in Morocco and discord in Portugal forced him to wait until 1441 for this information.

The war ended in a tragic defeat and the martyrdom of Henry's youngest brother, Fernando. Depressed but more fiercely devoted than ever to exploration, Prince Henry buried himself in his work at Sagres and concentrated on his plans.

In 1441 he sent his young chamberlain, Gonçalves, voyaging south to Rio do Ouro to hunt seals for their oil and skins. Rio do Ouro ("River of Gold") was a bay below Cape Bojador, mistaken by the Portuguese for a river and named for a legendary river of gold supposed to exist in Africa. Gonçalves persuaded his crew that it would be more interesting to hunt for people, and there his hunters caught their "game."

These were the first African slaves taken by modern Europeans. Azurara, in his *Chronicle of Guinea*, describes this fateful event, which was to lead in time to the transatlantic slave trade, the American Civil War, the formation of the Afro-Asian "bloc," and much of the strife in the world today.

Now it was . . . in this year 1441, when the affairs of this realm were somewhat more settled . . . that the Infant [Prince Henry] armed a little ship, of the which he made captain one Antão Gonçalves, his chamberlain, and a very young man; and the end of that voyage was . . . to ship a cargo of the skins and oil of . . . sea wolves [seals]. . . .

But when he had accomplished his voyage, as far as

concerned the chief part of his orders, Antão Gonçalves called to him Affonso Goterres, another groom
of the chamber, who was with him, and all the others
that were in the ship, being one and twenty in all, and
spoke to them in this wise:

"Friends and brethren! We have already got our
cargo . . . and we may well turn back . . . but I
would know from all whether . . . we should attempt something further. . . . O how fair a thing
it would be if we . . . were to meet with the good
luck to bring the first captives before the face of our
Prince. . . .

"I would fain go myself this next night with nine
men of you . . . along the river, to see if I find any
inhabitants. . . . And, if God grant us to encounter
them, the very least part of our victory will be the
capture of one of them, with the which the Infant
will feel no small content, getting knowledge by that
means of what kind are the other dwellers of this
land. . . ."

Gonçalves chose nine men, and they landed that night.
In the morning they marched inland about ten miles, and
then found footprints of forty or fifty men pointed back
toward the shore.

Gonçalves . . . said, "My friends . . . these men
are traveling to the place whence we have come, and
our best course would be to turn back toward them,

and perchance, on their return, some will separate themselves, or may be, we shall come up with them when they are laid down to rest. . . ."

And, returning toward the sea, when they had gone a short part of the way, they saw a naked man following a camel, with two assegais [spears] in his hand, and as our men pursued him there was not one who felt aught of his great fatigue.

But though he was only one . . . yet he had a mind to . . . defend himself as best he could. . . . But Affonso Goterres wounded him with a javelin, and this put the Moor in such fear that he threw down his arms like a beaten thing. . . .

And, as they were going on their way, they saw a black Mooress come along . . . and . . . they seized the Mooress . . .

An armed caravel, captained by Nuno Tristão, now unexpectedly joined Gonçalves at Rio do Ouro. Each ship sent eleven men on a second raid.

And so it chanced that in the night they came to where the natives lay scattered in two encampments. . . . The distance between the encampments was but small, and our men divided themselves into three parties, in order that they might the better hit upon them. . . .

And when our men had come nigh to them, they attacked them very lustily, shouting at the top of their voices, "Portugal" and "Santiago"; the fright of which so abashed the enemy, that . . . they began to fly without any order. . . .

Except indeed that the men made some show of defending themselves . . . especially one of them, who fought . . . with Nuno Tristão . . . till he received his death. And besides this one, whom Nuno Tristão slew . . . the others killed three and took ten prisoners, what of men, women and boys.

The Portuguese Change Their Minds

In his African voyages Prince Henry was seeking knowledge, conversions, and victory over the Moors. At first, however, although Henry used funds of the Knights of Christ, of which he was Grand Master, the man in the street criticized the project as a waste of money. What were Prince Henry's captains bringing back from Africa so far? Not gold but geography! What good was that?

Now Gonçalves and Tristão appeared with their slaves, plus a little gold dust Gonçalves had obtained as ransom for two captives. At this, as Azurara's *Chronicle of Guinea* narrates below, the man in the street decided to take a second look at Prince Henry's project.

Tristão immediately knighted Gonçalves there on the shore, for which reason the place was called "the Port of the Cavalier." Prince Henry was delighted with the captives, says Azurara, and his joy "was solely from that one holy purpose . . . to seek salvation for the lost souls of the heathen."

At the beginning of the colonization of the [Atlantic] islands, people murmured as greatly as if [Prince Henry] were spending some part of their property on it . . . and . . . declared his work . . . could never be accomplished at all. But after the Infant [Prince Henry] began to people those islands, and . . . after the fruits of those countries began to appear in Portugal . . . then those who had been foremost in complaint grew quiet, and with soft voices praised what they had so loudly . . . decried.

And just the same they did in the commencement of this conquest [of Africa]; for in the first years, seeing the . . . great expense, these busybodies . . . occupied themselves in discussing what they understood very little about; and the more slowly the results came in of the Infant's undertaking, the more loudly did they blame it . . . declaring that no profit would result from all this toil and expense.

But when they saw the first Moorish captives brought home, and the second cargo that followed these, they became already somewhat doubtful about the opinion they had at first expressed; and altogether renounced it when they saw the third consignment [of captives] that Nuno Tristão brought home. . . . And so they were forced to turn their blame into public praise. . . . And, as they saw the houses of others full to overflowing of male and female slaves . . . they . . . began to talk among themselves. . . .

And . . . the people of [Lagos, the seaport next to Sagres] were the first to move the Infant to give them license to go to that land whence came those Moorish captives.

The Slave Market at Lagos

The Portuguese now became greedy for profits from the slave trade. In the first half of the fifteenth century Portugal was suffering from a manpower shortage. Importing Berber (Moorish) and Negro slaves from Africa seemed a convenient way to provide laborers for the fields, make money, and at the same time get to heaven by converting pagans to Christianity.

Henry did not personally profit from the slave trade. Apparently he was able to accept it because he considered conversion to Christianity more important than freedom, because the slaves were treated fairly well in Portugal, and because the profit motive made seamen more eager to embark on exploring voyages under him. Henry subordinated everything to his passion for discovery.

In the fifteenth century there was also a shortage of gold in Portugal and throughout Europe. Prince Henry's chief commercial motive had been to tap the rich supply of African gold, which was brought across the Sahara in caravans from somewhere in the interior. In 1443 Nuno Tristão sailed south past sandy Cape Blanco ("Cape White") to the island of Arguim, well down the western bulge of Africa. Here Henry had a fort and factory (trading post) built, hoping to divert to Portuguese ships some of the goods usually carried north across the desert. Especially, the Portuguese hoped to obtain gold.

They did obtain melegueta pepper, gum, civet, and a little gold dust in exchange for cloths, linens, wheat, bowls, pots, combs, looking glasses, etc., but the great wealth taken in at Arguim consisted of slaves. At first by free-lance raids of their own, later by bartering their goods for Negro slaves supplied by Arab merchants, the Portuguese obtained 927 slaves before 1448, and after that a thousand slaves a year. Some of the goods they bartered were chains, rings, and fetters, to be used by the Arab merchants on future captives.

The slaves were carried from Arguim to the slave market at Lagos, Portugal, where those who had survived the trip were sold. The confusion and the misery of that slave market are expressed below in the most eloquent words Azurara ever wrote. He is describing, in his *Chronicle of Guinea*, the division on August 8, 1444, of 235 captives—the first large group brought back from Africa.

O, Thou heavenly Father . . . I pray Thee that my tears may not wrong my conscience; for it is not their religion but their humanity that maketh mine to weep in pity for their sufferings. And if the brute animals . . . understand the sufferings of their own kind, what wouldst Thou have my human nature to do on seeing before my eyes that miserable company? . . .

Very early in the morning, by reason of the heat, the seamen began to make ready their boats, and to take out those captives, and carry them on shore, as they were commanded. And these, placed all together in that field, were a marvelous sight; for amongst them were some white enough, fair to look upon, and well proportioned; others were less white like mulattoes; others again were as black as Ethiops, and so

ugly . . . as almost to appear . . . the images of a lower hemisphere.

But what heart could be so hard as not to be pierced with piteous feeling to see that company? For some kept their heads low and their faces bathed in tears, looking one upon another; others stood groaning very dolorously, looking up to the height of heaven . . . ; others struck their faces with the palms of their hands, throwing themselves at full length upon the ground; others made their lamentations in the manner of a dirge, after the custom of their country. And though we could not understand the words . . . the sound . . . right well accorded with the measure of their sadness.

But to increase their sufferings still more, there now arrived those who had charge of the division of the captives, and who began to separate one from another, in order to make an equal partition of the fifths; and then it was needful to part fathers from sons, husbands from wives, brothers from brothers. No respect was shown either to friends or relations, but each fell where his lot took him. . . .

And who could finish that partition without very great toil? for as often as they had placed them in one part the sons, seeing their fathers in another, rose with great energy and rushed over to them; the mothers clasped their other children in their arms, and threw themselves flat on the ground with them; receiving blows with little pity for their own flesh, if only they might not be torn from them.

And so troublously they finished the partition; for . . . the field was quite full of people, both from the town and from the surrounding . . . districts, who . . . [had come] for the sole purpose of beholding this novelty. And with what they saw, while some were weeping and others separating the captives, they caused . . . a [further] tumult. . . .

The Infant [Prince Henry] was there, mounted upon a powerful steed, and accompanied by his retinue, making distribution of his favors, as a man who sought to gain but small treasure from his share; for of the forty-six souls that fell to him as his fifth, he made a very speedy partition of these; for his chief riches lay in [the accomplishment of] his purpose; for he reflected with great pleasure upon the salvation of those souls that before were lost.

And certainly his expectation was not in vain; for . . . as soon as they understood our language they turned Christians with very little ado; and I who put together this history . . . saw in the town of Lagos boys and girls (the children and grandchildren of those first captives, born in this land) as good and true Christians as if they had directly descended, from the beginning of the dispensation of Christ, from those who were first baptized.

A Voyage to Africa

What was it like to go exploring in the service of Prince Henry? Fortunately we have a personal record of one voyage, made a few years later when the Portuguese had reached the "land of the real Negroes": Cape Verde, westernmost point of the African coast, and Guinea itself, with its fabled wealth of ivory, gold, and more slaves.

The voyage was made by Alvise da Cadamosto, a young Venetian who had sailed in his teens on Barbary galleys and achieved the rank of "noble bowman." Cadamosto was on his way from Italy to Flanders in a Venetian fleet when bad weather forced his ship to seek shelter at Cape St. Vincent. There the Venetian consul to Portugal suggested that he enlist under Prince Henry, as captains from as far away as Denmark had done.

Cadamosto was an alert observer of the businesslike Portuguese and the intense Prince Henry. Like many of his countrymen, he desired fame and riches—and he possessed youth and talent. It was not hard for him to reach a decision.

The selection below, from Cadamosto's *Voyages*, tells how he took the consul's advice. Cadamosto's descriptions of Africa are the most authentic and picturesque that have come down to us from the fifteenth century.

In the year of Our Lord 1454, I, Alvise Cadamosto, then aged about twenty-two years, found myself in our city of Venice. Having sailed to various parts of our Mediterranean Sea, I then determined to return to Flanders, where I had been once before, in the hope of profit. . . .

Cadamosto hoped to restore his father's fortunes, lost

through lawsuits and banishment from Venice. Before his downfall, the elder Cadamosto had been an important state official.

I made ready with what little money I had, and went aboard our fleet of Flanders galleys. . . . Sailing southward . . . we ultimately made the coast of Spain.

Contrary winds delayed the galleys at Cape St. Vincent . . . so that by chance I found myself at no great distance from the place where the Lord Infant Don Henry was lodged. . . . When he had news of us, he sent one of his secretaries . . . accompanied by a . . . Venetian . . . to our galleys with samples of sugar from the Isle of Madeira, dragon's blood [a resin] and other products of his domains and islands. . . .

He [Prince Henry's secretary] said that his lord had peopled newly discovered islands . . . caused seas to be navigated which had never before been sailed, and had discovered the lands of many strange races, where marvels abounded. Those who had been in these parts had wrought great gain among these new peoples. . . .

Hearing this, I determined . . . to go [sail in the service of Prince Henry]. . . . After many days he had a new caravel fitted out for me, of some ninety tons burden. . . . Furnished with all necessities, we set sail [for Africa] in God's name and with high hopes . . . on the 22 March 1455.

An Ocean of Sand

Cadamosto touched at Madeira and the Canaries, then doubled Cape Blanco and sailed along the Sahara Desert.

The Sahara stretches from the Atlantic to the Nile River, a distance equal to that between New York and California, and extends southward into the continent for 800 to 1,400 miles. Most of it is a stony, windswept waste—there are even 8,000-foot mountains, snow-topped in winter, in the middle of it—but what Cadamosto saw below Cape Blanco resembled a movie desert, a Hollywood setting for the Foreign Legion.

Scalloped dunes, sixty to seventy feet high, marched in waves down to the shore. Sand "smoked" from the tops of the dunes in the sea breeze, and the desert stretched east like an immense ocean itself, a dazzling white-gold under the glare of the African sun.

In Cadamosto's time, as today, the desert was thinly peopled with wandering Tuareg tribesmen. Cadamosto calls them "Arabs," a general term for the desert dwellers. Actually, the Tuaregs were Berbers, that is, the original, native inhabitants of North Africa who had been infiltrated by the conquering Mohammedan Arabs in the eleventh century. "Tuareg" is derived from an Arab verb meaning "to give up," and may have been applied to the Berbers because they "gave up" the Christianity they had received from the Romans earlier, replacing it with the new Moslem faith.

The Tuareg "Arabs" were a brown-skinned, black-haired people whose most striking habit was the wearing of the *litham* (cloth) over their faces, perhaps to protect their throats and lungs from sand. (But Cadamosto below gives a different reason.) They were called "The People of the Veil."

We set sail from [the Canary Islands] making due

south . . . and in a few days reached Cape Blanco about [570 miles] from the Canaries. . . .

Along the coast [as one sails] to Cape Blanco commences the sandy country which is the desert. . . . This desert the Berbers [natives] call Sahara ["Wilderness"]: on the south it marches with the Blacks of lower [Africa]: it is a very great desert, which takes well-mounted men fifty to sixty days to cross. . . . The boundary of this desert is on the Ocean Sea at the coast, which is everywhere sandy, white, arid, and all equally low-lying. . . .

[The inhabitants] are Mohammedans, and very hostile to Christians. They never remain settled, but are always wandering over these deserts. These are the men who go to the land of the Blacks, and also to our nearer Barbary. They . . . have many camels on which they carry brass and silver from Barbary and other things to Timbuktu and to the land of the Blacks. Thence they carry away gold and pepper, which they bring hither.

They are brown complexioned, and wear white cloaks edged with a red stripe; their women also dress thus. . . . On their heads the men wear turbans . . . and they always go barefooted. . . . They live on dates, barley, and camel's milk. . . . They are men who require little food and can withstand hunger. . . .

You should know that these people have no knowledge of any Christians except the Portuguese, against whom they have waged war for thirteen or fourteen years, many of them having been taken prisoners . . . and sold into slavery. It is asserted that when for the first time they saw sails, that is, ships, on the sea . . . they believed that they were great sea birds with white wings, which were flying, and had come from some strange place: when the sails were lowered for the landing, some of them, watching from far off, thought that the ships were fishes.

Others again said that they were phantoms that went by night, at which they were greatly terrified. The reason for this belief was because these caravels within a short space of time appeared at many places, where attacks were delivered, especially at night, by their crews. . . . Perceiving this, they said . . . "If these be human creatures, how can they travel so great a distance in one night . . . ?" Thus, as they did not understand the art of navigation, they all thought that the ships were phantoms. . . .

These same Azaneguys [Berbers] have a strange custom: they always wear a handkerchief on the head with a flap [veil] which they bring across the face, covering the mouth and part of the nose. For they say that the mouth is a brutish thing, that is always uttering wind and bad odors so that it should be kept covered, and not displayed.

The "Silent Trade"

As he sailed along the edge of the Sahara Desert, Cadamosto learned of the exchange of salt for gold, of how the Arabs traded their salt for gold produced by the Negroes to the south. Thus he gained information about the mysterious African gold trade that Prince Henry was eager to take part in.

As early as the fourteenth century a European map showed the Sahara region with the figure of a Negro monarch, enthroned, holding aloft a nugget of gleaming gold; yet because of the secrecy of the Moslem traders and their hostility toward Christians, Europeans knew even less about North African trade than they did about distant Asia. Cadamosto was the first to give them details about the gold trade.

The gold was mined by the Negroes chiefly in the Wangara fields, just south of the Sahara and not far inland from Cape Verde. They sank shafts seventeen to twenty-two feet deep into the earth, the women carrying away and washing the "dirt." Or they found gold in the rivers, in the deposits in river gravels, by diving during the low-water season. The Wangara fields were in the Negro country of Mali, which Cadamosto mentions.

The Mali Negroes exchanged their gold for salt brought from the central Sahara, down the caravan route to Timbuktu at the southern edge of the desert and then into their country. The salt was dug out of the sand by slaves of the Arabs in Taghaza, which was a "salt city": its houses and mosques were built of blocks of salt, roofed with camel skins.

Because of the hot, humid climate, the Mali Negroes desperately needed these Arab "salt tablets" in their diet—and, of course, the Arab traders wanted gold. A pound of salt was sometimes exchanged for a pound of gold. Today a pound of gold would buy a houseful of salt!

The Negroes of Mali used the salt themselves but also traded some of it with another tribe of Negroes. In his

Voyages Cadamosto describes the "silent trade" between the two Negro tribes who were too shy, or too fearful, to face each other.

There is a place called Taghaza . . . where a very great quantity of rock-salt is mined. Every year large caravans of camels belonging to the . . . Arabs and Azaneguys [Berbers] . . . carry it to Timbuktu; thence they go to Mali, the empire of the Blacks, where, so rapidly is it sold, within eight days of its arrival all is disposed of at a price of two to three hundred mitkals [25 to 37 ounces of gold] a load; then with the gold they return to their homes.

In this empire of Mali it is very hot, and the pasturage is very unsuitable for four-footed animals: so that of the majority which come with the caravans no more than twenty-five out of a hundred return. . . . Many also of the Arabs and Azaneguys sicken in this place and die, on account of the great heat. . . .

I inquired . . . what the merchants of Mali did with this salt, and was told that a small quantity is consumed in their country. Since it is . . . on the equinoctial [equator] . . . it is extremely hot at certain seasons of the year; this causes the blood to putrefy, so that were it not for this salt, they would die. The remedy they employ is as follows: they take a small piece of the salt, mix it in a jar with a little water, and drink it every day. They say that this saves them. . . .

You must know that when this salt is carried to Mali by camel it goes in large pieces. . . . Then at Mali, these blacks break it in smaller pieces, in order to carry it on their heads . . . until they reach certain waters. . . . Having reached these waters . . . they proceed in this fashion: all those who have the salt pile it in rows, each marking his own. Having made these piles, the whole caravan retires half a day's journey.

Then there come another race of blacks who do not wish to be seen or to speak. They arrive in large boats. . . . Seeing the salt, they place a quantity of gold opposite each pile, and then turn back, leaving salt and gold.

When they have gone, the Negroes who own the salt return: if they are satisfied with the quantity of gold, they leave the salt and retire with the gold. Then the blacks of the gold return, and remove those piles which are without gold. By the other piles of salt they place more gold, if it pleases them, or else they leave the salt.

In this way, by long and ancient custom, they carry on their trade without seeing or speaking to each other.

The Senegal—Boundary River

When we had passed in sight of this Cape Blanco, we sailed on our journey to the river called the Senegal, the first river of the Land of the Blacks, which debouches on this coast. This river separates the Blacks from the brown people called Azaneguys [Berbers], and also the dry and arid land, that is, the above-mentioned desert, from the fertile country of the Blacks.

The river is large, its mouth being over a mile wide, and quite deep. There is another mouth a little distance beyond, with an island between. . . . About a mile out to sea are shoals and broad sand banks. . . . From Cape Blanco . . . all the coast is sandy to within about twenty miles of the mouth [of the river]. . . .

It appears to me a very marvelous thing that beyond the river all men are very black, tall and big, their bodies well formed; and the whole country green, full of trees, and fertile: while on this side, the men are brownish . . . lean, ill-nourished, and small in stature: the country sterile and arid. This river is said to be a branch of the river Nile, of the four royal rivers.

Fifteenth century geographers called the Senegal "the western Nile" because they thought it was a branch of the Nile in Egypt. The Nile itself was supposed to be one of the four rivers flowing from the earthly paradise, which was located vaguely somewhere in the Far East. The other three rivers were the Euphrates, the Tigris, and the Phison.

Swimmers, Ships, and Moonlight Dances

The "Land of the Blacks" which Cadamosto now reached

is what most of us think of when we hear the word
"Africa": coastal, equatorial Africa—low, hot, humid,
with dense forests, thick undergrowth, broad rivers, primitive tribesmen, witch doctors, elephants, crocodiles, and
monkeys.

This is the Africa which the Moslem traders coming
down from the Sahara had not been able to penetrate,
but which the caravels of Prince Henry would explore
and reveal to the world.

("Africa" was originally the name of a Berber tribe; it
was given to the great continent, three times the size of
Europe, by the Romans. The Greeks called its inhabitants
men "with burnt faces.")

The selection which follows is from Cadamosto's
Voyages.

The faith of these first Blacks is Mohammedanism:
they are not however, as are the white Moors, very
resolute in this faith, especially the common people.
The chiefs adhere to the tenets of the Mohammedans
because they have around them priests of the Azaneguys [Berbers] or Arabs, who have reached this
country. . . .

These people dress thus: almost all constantly go
naked, except for a goatskin fashioned in the form
of drawers, with which they hide their shame. But the
chiefs and those of standing wear a cotton garment—
for cotton grows in these lands. Their women spin it
into cloth of a span in width. . . . These garments
are made to reach halfway down the thigh, with wide
sleeves to the elbow. They also wear breeches of this

cotton, which are tied across, and reach to the ankles. . . .

They are talkative, and never at a loss for something to say; in general they are great liars and cheats, but on the other hand, charitable, receiving strangers willingly, and providing a night's lodging and one or two meals without any charge. . . .

These same Blacks are the most expert swimmers in the world. . . . [Once] I asked these Blacks if there was anyone who could swim well and was bold enough to carry my letter to the ship, three miles off shore. At once many said they were.

As the sea was high and there was much wind, I said it appeared to me almost impossible that any man could succeed—principally because at a bowshot from the shore there were sandbanks and likewise farther out to sea at another bowshot more banks, between which the current was so strong, now rising, now falling, that it would be very difficult for any swimmer to keep from being swept away. The sea was breaking . . . heavily over these banks. . . .

However that might be, two Negroes presented themselves as willing to go. . . . I cannot narrate the difficulties they encountered in attempting to pass those banks in that sea. Whenever they disappeared from sight for a considerable time I thought that they must have been drowned. At last one could no longer withstand such buffeting from the waves, so many were breaking over him, and turned back; but the other stood firm, and fought for a long hour on the bank. In the end, he crossed it, and bore the letter to the ship, returning with a reply. . . .

These Negroes, men and women, crowded to see me as though I were a marvel. . . . They marveled no less at my clothing than at my white skin. My clothes were after the Spanish fashion, a doublet of black damask, with a short cloak of gray wool over it. They examined the woolen cloth, which was new to them, and the doublet with much amazement: some touched my hands and limbs, and rubbed me with their spittle to discover whether my whiteness was dye or flesh. Finding that it was flesh, they were astounded. . . .

They were also struck with admiration by the construction of our ship, and by her equipment— mast, sails, rigging, and anchors. They were of opinion that the portholes in the bows of ships were really eyes by which the ships saw whither they were going over the sea. They said we must be great wizards, almost the equal of the devil, for men that journey by land have difficulty in knowing the way from place to place, while we journeyed by sea, and . . . remained out of sight of land for many days, yet knew which direction to take, a thing only possible through the power of the devil. This appeared so to them because they do not understand the art of navigation. . . .

They also marveled much on seeing a candle burn-
ing in a candlestick, for here they do not know how
to make any other light than that of a fire. To them
the sight of the candle . . . was beautiful and
miraculous. . . .

The women of this country are very pleasant and
lighthearted, ready to sing and to dance, especially
the young girls. They dance, however, only at night
by the light of the moon. Their dances are very different from ours.

The Southern Cross

As the Portuguese caravels with the great red crosses
painted on their sails forged southward, the North Star
sank lower and lower in the northern sky. But directly
south, also low on the horizon but rising, the seamen now
saw a cross in the sky: the beautiful constellation known
as the Southern Cross. Cadamosto calls it the "southern
wain," making it correspond to the Big Dipper ("Charles's
Wain").

Cadamosto's diagram, from his *Voyages*, shows the six
bright stars of the constellation. The upright, or long, part
of the cross points toward the south celestial pole. The
Southern Cross may be seen only as far north as southern
Florida or Texas.

During the days we spent at the mouth of this
river [the Gambia, below Cape Verde], we saw the
pole star once only; it appeared very low down over
the sea, therefore we could see it only when the
weather was very clear. It appeared about a third of a
lance above the horizon.

We also had sight of six stars low down over the sea, clear, bright, and large. By the compass, they stood due south, in the following fashion—

               ✳

   ✳   ✳   ✳   ✳

            ✳

This we took to be the southern wain, though we did not see the principal star, for it would not have been possible to sight it unless we had lost the North Star.

Cadamosto found little of the gold he was seeking and soon returned to Portugal. The next year, 1456, he made a second voyage to the Gambia. On the way he was blown off his course, and on the third day of the storm the sailors all shouted "Land! Land!" as they sighted two large islands. These turned out to be part of the Cape Verde Islands, an arid, tropical archipelago of ten islands on which Cadamosto found nothing but "doves, strange species of birds, and large shoals of fishes."

The Cape Verdes, three hundred miles west of Africa, are the only island group in the eastern Atlantic which almost certainly had not been discovered before the fifteenth century. The Portuguese began to colonize them in 1461.

In 1460 Prince Henry the Navigator died. The king, says a contemporary, "made great mourning on the death of a Prince so mighty, who had sent out so many fleets . . . and had fought so constantly . . . for the Faith."

Medieval crusader and Renaissance man-of-science combined, Prince Henry had changed the world by his bold plans for discovery. One scholar suggests that just as Portuguese ships rounding Cape St. Vincent used to lower their sails in deference to the saint, so our steamers passing the same cape might dip their flags to honor a prince who opened half the world to exploration.

Southward Toward the Cape

Africa is a huge continent, shaped roughly like a thick, upside down L (⌐). The first problem of the Portuguese had been to sail around the upper part, the bulge of North Africa. For nearly ten years after Prince Henry's death they did not get past Sierra Leone ("Lion Mountains") at the edge of Guinea, a range whose frequent thunder sounded like a cageful of lions.

Then, in return for a five-year monopoly (1469–74) of the Guinea trade, an enterprising Lisbon merchant named Fernão Gomes sent his ships beyond Guinea to where the African coast turns south again. One of his most valuable imports was the civet cat, whose secretion is used in perfumes. In 1473 Gomes's vessels crossed the equator.

War between Portugal and Spain (1475–79) halted exploration. Then, in 1481, a new king, John II, came to the throne. John II was a man of medium height but com-

manding presence. Clad in red velvet suit, black hose, and white shirt, a dagger (which he knew well how to use) in his belt, he looked every inch "the Perfect Prince."

John II had the persistence and imagination of his great-uncle, Prince Henry, along with more money to spend and an even sterner temperament. He, too, was determined to reach India.

First, to give Portugal control of the rich Guinea Gold Coast, he had a powerful fortress built at Elmina ("The Mine") on that coast. Among those who sailed to build this fort may have been a tall, red-haired Genoese, a captain who was always poring over maps, annotating books of geography, and vociferously arguing that the shortest route to Asia was *west* across the Ocean Sea. This was Christopher Columbus, preparing himself for his great voyage.

In the same year, 1482, John II ordered a commoner about whom very little is known, Diogo Cão, to sail farther south than any European had yet gone. After crossing the equator, the humble but competent Cão coasted along fine red cliffs until he encountered a flood of brown water pouring from a tremendous river. He landed on the south bank and exchanged cloth for ivory brought by the astonished natives.

The natives informed Cão that the river, seven miles wide at its mouth, was called the *Nzadi* (corrupted by the Portuguese to the "Zaire").

Here Cão unloaded one of his new markers, a marble pillar six feet high with a cross on top, and planted it. The pillar (*padrão*) contained an inscription giving the names of King John II and Diogo Cão, and the date; it would be more permanent than the wooden crosses or tree carvings used before.

Cão called the marker "The Pillar of St. George" and the river "The River of the Pillar" (*Rio do Padrão*). But this river, which made the sea fresh for nine miles off-shore, is now known as the Congo. The natives were the Mani-Congo.

Cão sailed a short way up the Congo and left several of his seamen there to find a powerful king said to live in the interior. Then he returned to the coast and continued his voyage as far as Cape St. Mary, in 13° south latitude, where he planted a *padrão* with the following inscription:

> Year of the creation of the world 6681, year of the birth of Our Lord Jesus Christ 1482, the very high, very excellent and powerful prince King John second of Portugal sent to have this land discovered and these *padrões* placed by Diogo Cão, squire of his household.

When Cão returned to Lisbon, King John "separated him from the common herd" by a patent of nobility and granted him a coat of arms displaying two shining *padrões*.

In 1485 Diogo Cão, no longer a commoner but a noble-man, went back to the Congo, recovered the men he had left on the first voyage, and took his ships a hundred miles up the great stream through a fearful whirlpool known as "Hell's Caldron," where he carved his name and those of his companions on a rock. Then he sailed all the way to Cape Cross (22° south latitude), where he planted his last *padrão* and, according to one source, died.

But look at a map of Africa. Cape Cross is less than eight hundred miles from the Cape of Good Hope. In five years' time Diogo Cão had discovered as much of the African coast as had been explored in the preceding twenty years.

Suddenly the lateen sails of the caravels were wings. The slaves and gold of Guinea were left behind in pursuit of an idea, Prince Henry's idea, as the Portuguese reached the threshold of the East, and Dias and Vasco da Gama awaited their call on stage.

3
The Sea Road to India

As Prester John, I am lord of lords, I surpass under heaven in riches and in virtue and power all other kings who are upon the whole earth.

—Letter of Prester John

A Secret Mission

Throughout the Middle Ages, Christendom was hemmed in—by ice to the north, by the Ocean Sea to the west, and by barbarians or Moslems to the east and south. But Christians could dream, not only of a better life in the world to come, but of an earthly paradise here. When frosts were too biting, feudal lords too harsh, invasion or the Black Death imminent, men spoke of the marvelous kingdom of Prester John.

Was not the Prester himself, who was both priest and king, supposed to have written to the Byzantine emperor: "Honey flows in our land, and milk everywhere abounds. . . . There are no poor among us. Thieves and robbers are not found in our land, nor . . . is . . . strife among us, but our people have abundance of riches"?

It was said to be a land of wonders. One of its rivers contained "emeralds, sapphires, carbuncles, topazes . . . and many other precious stones." Ants the size of dogs dug for gold. Tasty fish swam in a sea of sand. If you climbed into a stone shell shaped like a wading pool you would be cured of any sickness, and if you took three drinks of a fountain which changed its flavor every hour you would "remain as if of the age of thirty-two years as long as [you] live." Ponce de Leon might have been looking for Prester John in Florida.

That, of course, was the problem: where was the kingdom of Prester John to be found? Europe desperately wanted to know, because such a ruler would make a powerful ally against the Moslems.

"Our magnificence dominates the Three Indias and extends . . . through the desert to the rising sun," Prester John was supposed to have stated in his *Letter* of 1165. Unfortunately this famous *Letter* was a forgery; an anonymous European prankster wrote it. Yet there *were* scattered Christian communities in Asia and an ancient but little known Christian kingdom, Ethiopia, in Africa.

When Europeans became skeptical about the *Letter*, they still continued their search for Prester John.

In the thirteenth century, when Mongol conquests temporarily opened Asia to Christians (the Mongols welcomed merchants and missionaries), Marco Polo sought him among the Mongol khans. In the fourteenth century, after the Mongols adopted Mohammedanism, Christians looked for the Prester in Africa. Although legend gave him the power to change the course of the Nile and still spoke of him as descended from one of the Three Wise Men, Prester John gradually became identified with the reigning monarch of Ethiopia.

In 1487 King John II of Portugal summoned two experienced travelers for briefing on a dangerous secret mission involving Prester John. King John would send these travelers, who spoke fluent Arabic, overland to seek Prester John at the same time that he dispatched Bartholomew Dias on a sea expedition to find the end of Africa. Dias was to discover the way *into* the Indian Ocean, while the overland scouts, Covilhan and Paiva, learned what route should be followed *through* this Ocean to reach India. King John would thus secure the information the Portuguese needed to attain their goal.

The selection below, from Alvares's *True Relation of the Lands of the Prester John*, published in 1540, tells how Covilhan and Paiva carried out their assignment.

The King spoke to [Pero de Covilhan] in great secrecy, telling him that he expected a great service of him. . . . This service was that he and another companion, who was named Afonso de Paiva, should both go to discover and learn about the Prester John and whether he bordered on the sea, and where pepper and cinnamon is to be found, and the other spices which from these parts went to Venice through the countries of the Moors. . . .

They were dispatched . . . on May 7, 1487 . . . [with] a chart, taken from the map of the world . . . [which] had been made very secretly. . . . One of them could go to Ethiopia to see the Prester John's country and see whether in his seas there was any knowledge of a passage to the western seas. . . .

They passed over to Alexandria in a ship . . . and in order to pass as merchants, they bought a great deal of honey. . . . Here both the companions fell ill of fevers; and all their honey was taken by the [Governor] of Alexandria, thinking that they were dying, [but] God gave them health. . . . [Then] they bought other merchandise and went to Cairo . . . [and] to Aden . . . [and there] separated. . . . Afonso de Paiva set out for . . . Ethiopia, and Pero de Covilhan decided for India . . . agreeing that at a certain time they should both meet in Cairo. . . .

And Pero de Covilhan . . . came to Cananore, and thence to Calicut. He saw the great quantity of ginger and pepper that originated there and heard that the cloves and cinnamon were brought from distant countries. From there he . . . returned . . . to Cairo where he spent a long while in search of his companion, and he found that he was dead.

When he was about to set out . . . to Portugal, he had news that there were two Portuguese Jews who were . . . looking for him; and by great cunning they knew each other, and when they had met, they gave him letters from the King of Portugal. . . .

Their contents were, that if all the things for which they [Covilhan and Paiva] had come were seen, found, and known, that they should return . . . [but] if all were not found . . . they were to send word of what they had found, and to labor to learn the rest . . . chiefly . . . to go and . . . learn about the great King Prester John. . . .

[Covilhan] at once wrote . . . how he had discovered cinnamon and pepper in the city of Calicut, and that cloves came from beyond, but that all could be had there; and that he had been in . . . Cananore, Calicut, and Goa, all on the coast, and to this they could well navigate by . . . the seas of Guinea, making for the coast of Sofala [East Africa], to which he had also gone, or a great island which the Moors call the Island of the Moon [Madagascar] . . . that from each of these lands one could fetch the coast of Calicut.

Having sent this message to the King by [one] Jew . . . Pero de Covilhan went with the other Jew . . . to Ormuz, and left him there, and turned back and . . . traveled . . . until he reached the Prester John.

The information Covilhan sent to King John II was used by Vasco da Gama in his voyage. Covilhan was "given a wife with very great riches and possessions" in Ethiopia, but he was such a valuable assistant to the King of Ethiopia that he was not permitted to return to Portugal. Alvares found him hale and hearty at age seventy-four, a wise counselor, surrounded by his dark, clear-eyed sons.

Around the Cape of Storms

The Cape of Good Hope has been called the point where one world ends and another begins. Until 1488, however, this majestic headland dividing East and West was not known for certain to exist. For seventy years Portuguese mariners had been sailing farther and farther south looking for the end of Africa but not finding it.

Phoenician merchant ships, like baskets with square sails, were said to have gone from the Red Sea around Africa to Gibraltar about 600 B.C.; on the other hand, Ptolemy taught that the Indian Ocean was landlocked, with no entrance from the Atlantic, and in 1291 a Genoese attempt to round Africa had failed. Prince Henry's dreams and King John II's plans might be in vain, as were later efforts to find a northwest passage through America to Asia.

In August, 1487, just two months after Covilhan and Paiva had departed overland to seek Prester John, Bartholomew Dias sailed from Lisbon under orders to settle once for all the question of the existence of a sea route around Africa. He was also to land captive Negro women along the coast with a message for Prester John, in case that elusive ruler turned out to be somewhere in southwest Africa instead of in the parts Covilhan and Paiva would visit.

Bartholomew Dias was a skillful navigator, experienced in the Guinea trade, courageous and loyal (like Hamlet's friend Horatio). His fleet consisted of two caravels (the *Christovão* and the *St. Pantaleão*) and a storeship; he was furnished with ample provisions and three *padrões*.

By January, 1488, Dias had left his storeship in a safe harbor below the Congo and was sailing far south of the most distant point hitherto reached. A desolate coast of sandhills was on his left, but still the wall of Africa stretched ahead, unbroken.

Suddenly a gale arose, and the caravels plunged in heavy seas. Sails were torn to shreds. For thirteen days, in darkness, the two small ships were driven straight toward the Antarctic. The sailors were in "mortal fear."

The gale blew itself out, and Dias steered east, thinking he would soon strike the coast, but no land appeared. Then he sailed north. On this course, after covering several hundred miles, the weary crews at last sighted land—land which slanted not south but east northeast.

Dias and his men stared, astonished, at the curve of Mossel Bay. Slowly the truth dawned: they had rounded Africa in the storm!

Immediately Dias wished to sail on; but only a few days later his worn crews began to protest. After landing at Mossel Bay for water and being pelted with stones by the inhospitable native Hottentots, one of whom they killed, they did sail as far as Cape Padrone (named for the *padrão* planted there) and the Great Fish River.

Then Dias had to yield to the pleas of his men and turn back; his spirits were high, but he was not ruthless enough to cow his crews. As he sailed past his pillar of St. Gregory, at Cape Padrone, he "took leave of it as from a beloved son whom he never expected to see again."

On the homeward voyage Dias saw the Cape itself and named it the "Cape of Storms." He picked up the survivors of the crew he had left with his storeship nine months earlier (one of them died of joy at seeing the caravels) and reached Lisbon in December, 1488.

Christopher Columbus witnessed Dias's return from his voyage, one of the greatest voyages in history, which ended Columbus's hopes of sailing west for Portugal. John II knew now that he could reach India by the eastern route. Apparently the king considered Dias's "Cape of Storms" unlucky, because he changed it to the "Cape of Good Hope," i.e., an omen of good hope for reaching India. He suppressed all accounts of this crucial voyage.

As for Dias, he received no great reward and was left behind when Vasco da Gama finally set sail. Dias, says a Portuguese historian, "saw the land of India, but, like Moses and the promised land, did not enter in."

Vasco da Gama Takes Command

John II was now on fire with eagerness to reach India. With Bartholomew Dias he discussed the best type of ship to use, and accepted Dias's suggestion that the traditional caravel be changed into a *nao*, with high bluff bows, higher bulwarks, and a broad beam, to withstand the "black tempests" of the Cape. The king even made a crucial improvement himself by having a lower gundeck built, with openings called *puertas* ("doors"—portholes) through which cannon could be discharged. But John II died in 1495, before the fleet could sail.

His successor was Manuel the Fortunate, a good administrator who was to carry out John's plans. As commander of the expedition, Manuel chose not the faithful veteran Dias but a thirty-seven-year-old nobleman—a man of action with a reputation as a daredevil: Vasco da Gama.

Vasco da Gama had grown up in Sines, a sunny fishing village south of Lisbon. Here he and his brothers learned to swim, fish, and sail. Later Vasco went inland to study mathematics and navigation at Évora, then entered the king's service. He was a high-spirited, persistent youth who became as skilled in navigation as the most experienced pilot.

The new captain-major (commander) now made a striking appearance. A rather thickset man of medium height, with a black spade beard and weathered, brick-red face, Vasco da Gama stood with shoulders squared and jaw clenched as though no hurricane of the Ocean Sea could make him budge an inch. Once when the police stopped him at night in a narrow street and asked for his identity, Vasco kept his face muffled, cried "I am no criminal!" and strode haughtily away. Dias's men had forced Dias to turn back after rounding Africa, but the devil himself would not keep Vasco da Gama from his goal.

Indeed, Vasco da Gama seemed to have a compulsion to impose his will upon others. He was given to unpredictable outbursts of anger and cruelty, yet was struck dumb with grief, on the return voyage, when his gentle brother Paul died. Paul was perhaps the only person Vasco ever loved. A strange man, Vasco, feared but respected by his crews—a man of suspicion, iron discipline, and accomplishment.

In the selection below, the Portuguese historian Gaspar Corrêa describes how King Manuel chose Vasco da Gama. The passage is from Corrêa's *Lendas da India*—"Legends," or "Records," of India, a history of Portuguese Asia, written 1530–63.

Whilst these things were being thus prepared, the king was full of care both day and night, as to whom he should trust this so great enterprise; he was always praying the Lord, that . . . He would be pleased to show him the men whom it would please Him to send upon this voyage. . . .

Many days passed thus, and one day the king sitting in his hall of business at a table with his officers, giving orders, by chance the king raised his eyes, and Vasco da Gama happened to cross through the hall: he was a gentleman of the household, and of noble lineage, son of Estevan da Gama. . . .

This Vasco da Gama was a discreet man, of good understanding, and of great courage for any good deed. The king setting eyes upon him, his heart was transported, and he called him, and he kneeled before the king, who said to him: "I should rejoice if you would undertake a service which I require of you in which you must labor much."

He kissed his hand, saying: "Sire, I am a servant for any labor that may be, since my service is required, which I will perform so long as my life lasts."

At which the king rose up, and went to sit at a table which was set out in the hall for dinner, and whilst there he said to Vasco da Gama that it was his will that he should go in those ships where he would send him, that it was an affair upon which he was much bent, and . . . that he should make ready.

To this, Vasco da Gama replied that his soul was in readiness, and that there was nothing to detain him from embarking at once.

When the king had finished dining he withdrew to his chamber, and asked of Vasco da Gama if he had any brother. He answered that he had three, one a lad, another who was studying to be a priest, and another older, and that all were men very ready to serve in anything that was committed to them.

The king said to him: "Call him to go with you in one of the two ships, and do you choose the one you like best, in which you shall carry my standard; for you shall be the captain-major of the others."

After preparations were completed, Vasco da Gama and his captains knelt before King Manuel, who declared that he ordered them to discover India in order to spread the Christian faith and to acquire riches for Portugal. He presented Vasco with a white silk banner of the Knights of Christ, with a copy of Covilhan's report about the East, and with letters to the King of Calicut—and to Prester John.

A Dire Prophecy

On July 8, 1497, the mudflats that lined the estuary of the Tagus River below Lisbon were covered with people, standing bareheaded in the blazing sunshine. From the small chapel of St. Mary of Bethlehem, built by Prince Henry, came a procession: priests and friars chanting a litany, then Vasco da Gama, his captains and his seamen, each bearing a lighted candle.

Slowly they moved away from the chapel, where Vasco da Gama had spent the night in prayer, toward the shore and the longboats waiting to carry them out to four high-castled black ships riding at anchor.

A deep sigh ran through the assembled friends and relatives. Although the day was clear, the sea blue, they could

not speak because of fear and grief. Suddenly they burst into loud groans.

The great Portuguese poet Luis de Camoens, who himself served in the East half a century later, has expressed the foreboding spirit of this departure. In his epic *The Lusiads* (*Os Lusiadas*), which tells the story of Vasco da Gama's voyage, Camoens introduces an imaginary "old man of Belem" who makes a dire prophecy just as the sailors embark. ("Belem" is Portuguese for "Bethlehem.")

The old man's prophecy is given below. Counselors of both John II and Manuel the Fortunate had given much the same advice the old man gave, warning that Portugal lacked the manpower to carry through ambitious plans for empire in the East. But the Portuguese kings rejected the advice.

The Lusiads means "the sons of Lusus," Lusus being a companion of the Greek god Bacchus and the mythical first settler of Portugal. Actually poets invented the name and character of Lusus on the basis of the authentic name (Lusitanians) of the original primitive inhabitants of the country (see p. xv).

But an old man of venerable air,
Who on the seafront stood among the crowd,
Turned his eyes toward us with a steady stare
And thrice his head as one in grief he bowed.
We on the water heard him clearly there,
For the voice charged with grief was somewhat loud.
With wisdom only to experience due,
Out of his much-tried breast these words he drew:

"Glory of empire! Most unfruitful lust
After the vanity that men call fame! . . .

"What new disasters dost thou now prepare
Against these kingdoms and against their seed?
What peril and what death for them to bear,
Under some mighty name, hast thou decreed?
What mines of gold now dost thou promise fair?
What kingdoms?—promise lightly made indeed!
What fame dost thou propose? What legend glorious?
What palm? What triumph? And what war
   victorious? . . .

"Wilt thou raise up the foeman in the gate,
While seeking out another worlds away,
Whereby unpeopled is the ancient state,
Weakened afar, and falling to decay?
Wilt thou rush on unknown ill and dubious fate,
That Fame may flatter thee and great things say,
Calling thee Lord, with plenteous plaudits dinned,
Of Araby, Ethiopia, Persia, Ind?"

The "old man of Belem," a Portuguese "Ancient Mariner," may have suggested to Melville the character Elijah, who in *Moby Dick* makes a grim prophecy as the *Pequod* sails.

Camoens's own life contains material for another epic. He was the first great writer to travel below the equator, the first to describe authentic sea life (such as the changing of the watch, a hurricane, scurvy, a water spout, etc.). He could neither resist a pretty face nor refuse a challenge to a duel.

In 1547, at age twenty-three, he was exiled from Portugal for falling in love with a beautiful, high-born lady. He lost an eye fighting in Morocco, survived a hurricane rounding the Cape of Good Hope, and held for a while an important government position in the East. In the East, also, he wrote his epic, had a love affair with a dark-haired Chinese girl, was shipwrecked off the mouth of the Mekong River and swam ashore holding his manuscript of *The Lusiads* above his head, and was imprisoned for debt. He returned to Portugal impoverished, published his epic (1572) for a small sum, and died as the Spanish troops entered Lisbon (1580) to bring Portugal temporarily under Spanish rule.

The nation of Portugal is the real hero of Camoens's poem, and of his heart. In his last letter, written just before his death, he said, "I loved my country so much that I shall die with her."

On Shipboard

Vasco da Gama and his men faced a trip of great discomfort as well as peril. Lest the ships be endangered, galley fires were doused whenever the wind became strong, so that for days at a stretch the crews ate uncooked food; at such times, if they were in the colder latitudes, the men also suffered from the freezing weather.

Toilet facilities were primitive, privacy was nonexistent, ship's surgeons were paid (and worth) less than carpenters, and the food was often unspeakable. Everyone tapped his biscuit against the table before eating it, to knock the worms out. (If no weevils fell out, it was a sign that the bread was really bad—even the worms wouldn't have it!)

An account of life on shipboard is given by Alexandro Valignano in the selection below. Valignano sailed in a Portuguese ship to India in the latter part of the sixteenth century; we can be sure that da Gama's men endured hardships at least as great as the ones described here.

The perils and hardships suffered on this expedition [to India] are very extensive and terrifying. The first hardship is lack of accommodation. True, the ships are large and powerful, but so packed with passengers, merchandise and provisions that there is little room left for anyone to move about, and the ordinary people aboard, for whose comfort there is no arrangement whatever, must stand all day on deck in the blazing sun and sleep there somehow all night in the cold. On the other hand, the berths put at the disposal of noble or wealthy persons are so low, so narrow, so confined, that it is all a man can do to fit himself into them.

The second hardship has to do with food and drink. Though his Highness the King provides daily rations of biscuit, meat, fish, water and wine sufficient to keep the passengers alive, the meat and fish are so salty, and the provision of utensils to collect the rations so inadequate, that the suffering on this account, especially among the soldiers, beggars description.

The third hardship among the general run of the voyagers is due to their being poor and happy-go-lucky. They set out with insufficient clothing, the little they bring soon rots on their backs, and they suffer dreadfully in lower latitudes, both from the cold and from the stench of their rags.

The fourth hardship is caused by the calms off the Guinea Coast, which may last for forty, fifty or sixty days. During that time the passengers almost sweat their souls out and suffer torments from the heat beyond the power of my pen to set forth.

The fifth hardship, and the worst of any, is the lack of water. During much of the voyage, the water doled out in the daily ration is so foul and malodorous that it is impossible to bear the stench of it, and the passengers have to put a piece of cloth before their mouths to filter off the corruption. This liquid is distributed only once a day, and many fail to get their portion through having no jugs in which to collect it. Others drink their entire ration at one gulp, the result being that large numbers die of thirst.

The sixth hardship results from disease of every description among the passengers, who suffer a thousand miseries before dying or recovering. The King appoints a surgeon to each ship, but he and his remedies soon cease to be of any use.

South with the Trade Winds

Vasco da Gama's four ships were the *naos St. Gabriel* and *St. Raphael* (both 100–200 tons), the caravel *Berrio* (50 tons), and an unnamed storeship (200 tons). Under their clouds of white canvas, logging an average forty-four miles a day, they sailed for the Orient, as adventurous as pioneers crossing the prairies to California.

No doubt the crews had misgivings, especially when Vasco da Gama, after leaving the Canaries and coasting along Guinea for a short distance, changed his course to south and then southwest, sailing into the unknown reaches of the "Green Sea of Darkness." Seamen glanced uneasily at their commander, who stood rigid, arms crossed, on the poop of the *St. Gabriel*, a velvet cap tugged down on his forehead. They had expected to voyage close to Africa, not steer away from it. Each evening at sunset they sang the Latin hymn to the Blessed Virgin Mary, the *Salve Regina*, more fervently than ever.

Vasco da Gama sailed in a great half circle which bent out toward Brazil, then back toward the bottom of Africa. He did this to avoid the doldrums (windless areas) of the Gulf of Guinea and the opposing southeast trade winds. When he reached 30° south latitude, his course was almost due east, and he picked up strong westerly winds which sped him on his way.

By sheer intuition, or perhaps on a hint from Dias, he had discovered the best route from Europe to India for sailing vessels, the one recommended today by both the British Admiralty and the United States Hydrographic Office. As we will see, Vasco da Gama's suggesting this course to Cabral, commander of the second expedition to India, led to the accidental discovery of Brazil.

Vasco da Gama's fleet was well equipped with food supplies and armaments, including cannon, but its trade goods were poorly chosen for the East. Glass beads, tin jewelry, little "tinkle bells," cheap cotton cloth, basins, and red hats fascinated the primitive Negroes of West Africa but would be contemptuously rejected when the fleet reached East Africa and India.

One hundred and seventy men sailed from Lisbon; two years later fewer than half of them would return.

An anonymous Portuguese on the *St. Raphael*, commanded by Paul da Gama, kept a *Log-Book* which has been described as "a plain, unadorned . . . [but] powerful description of a mighty undertaking." This *Log-Book*, written during or just after the trip, was not published until 1838. The selection below describes the voyage through the Atlantic.

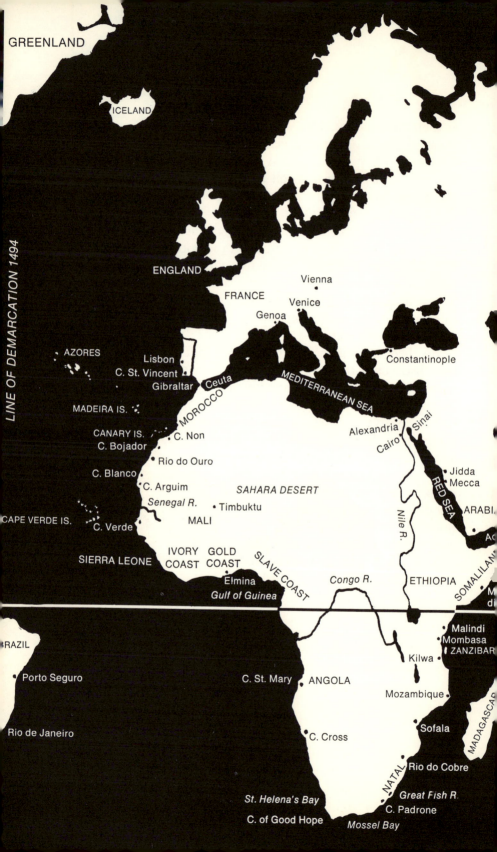

GREENLAND

ICELAND

LINE OF DEMARCATION 1494

ENGLAND

Vienna

FRANCE

Venice

Genoa

Constantinople

AZORES

Lisbon

C. St. Vincent

Gibraltar   Ceuta

MEDITERRANEAN SEA

MADEIRA IS.

MOROCCO

Alexandria   Sinai

CANARY IS.   C. Non

Cairo

C. Bojador

Jidda
Mecca

Rio do Ouro

C. Blanco

SAHARA DESERT

C. Arguim

RED SEA   ARABI.

Senegal R.   • Timbuktu

Ad

CAPE VERDE IS.

Nile R.

C. Verde   MALI

SIERRA LEONE   IVORY   GOLD

COAST   COAST   SLAVE COAST

Congo R.   ETHIOPIA

SOMALILAN.

Elmina   *Gulf of Guinea*

M
di

RAZIL

Malindi
Mombasa
ZANZIBAR

Porto Seguro

Kilwa

C. St. Mary   ANGOLA

Mozambique

Rio de Janeiro

Sofala

MADAGASCAR

C. Cross

NATAL   Rio do Cobre

St. Helena's Bay   *Great Fish R.*

C. Padrone

C. of Good Hope   *Mossel Bay*

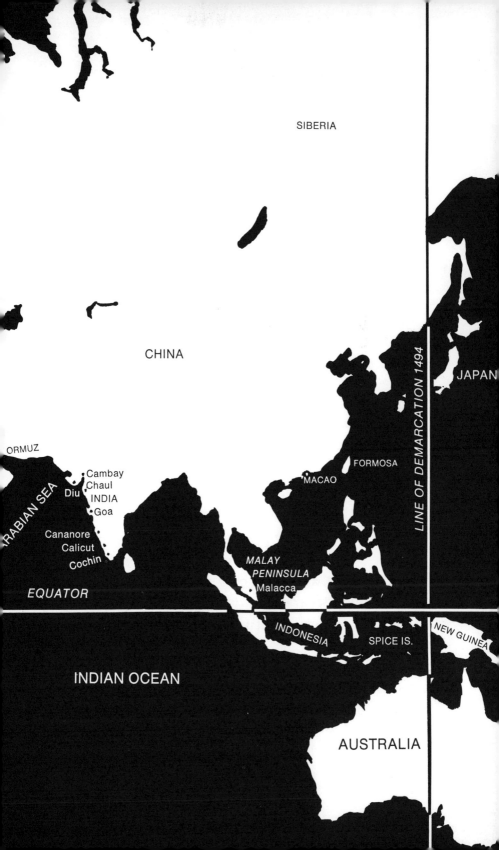

SIBERIA

CHINA

JAPAN

ORMUZ

Cambay
Chaul
Diu   INDIA
Goa

ARABIAN SEA

Cananore
Calicut
Cochin

FORMOSA

MACAO

LINE OF DEMARCATION 1494

EQUATOR

MALAY
PENINSULA
Malacca

INDONESIA

SPICE IS.

NEW GUINEA

INDIAN OCEAN

AUSTRALIA

In the name of God. Amen!

In the year 1497 King Dom Manuel, the first of that name in Portugal, dispatched four vessels to make discoveries and go in search of spices. Vasco da Gama was the captain-major of these vessels; Paul da Gama, his brother, commanded one of them, and Nicolas Coelho another.

We left [Lisbon] on Saturday, July 8, 1497. May God our Lord permit us to accomplish this voyage in his service. Amen!

On the following Saturday [July 15] we sighted the Canaries, and in the night passed to the lee of Lançarote [one of the Canaries]. During the following night, at break of day [July 16] we made the Terra Alta [West Africa], where we fished for a couple of hours, and in the evening, at dusk, we were off the Rio do Ouro [West Africa].

The fog during the night grew so dense that Paul da Gama lost sight of the captain-major, and when day broke [July 17] we saw neither him nor the other vessels. We therefore made sail for the Cape Verde islands, as we had been instructed to do in case of becoming separated.

On the following Saturday [July 22], at break of day, we sighted the Ilha do Sal [one of the Cape Verdes], and an hour afterward discovered three vessels, which turned out to be the storeship and the vessels commanded by Nicolas Coelho and Bartholomew Dias, the last of whom sailed in our company as far as The Mine [Elmina, West Africa]. They, too, had lost sight of the captain-major.

Having joined company, we pursued our route, but the wind fell, and we were becalmed until Wednesday [July 26]. At ten o'clock on that day we sighted the captain-major, about five leagues ahead of us, and having got speech with him in the evening we gave expression to our joy by many times firing off our bombards [cannon] and sounding the trumpets.

The day after this, a Thursday [July 27], we arrived at the island of Santiago [largest of the Cape Verdes], and joyfully anchored in the bay of Santa Maria [at Santiago], where we took on board meat, water and wood, and did . . . much-needed repairs to our yards.

On Thursday, August 3, we left in an easterly direction. On August 18, when about two hundred leagues from Santiago, going south, the captain-major's main yard broke, and we lay to under foresail and lower mainsail for two days and a night.

On the 22nd [of October], when going S. by W., we saw many birds resembling herons. On the approach of night they flew vigorously to the S.S.E., as if making for the land. On the same day, being then quite eight hundred leagues out at sea [from Santiago], we saw a whale.

On Friday, October 27, the eve of St. Simon and Jude, we saw many whales, as also . . . seals.

On Wednesday, November 1, the day of All Saints, we perceived many indications of the neighborhood of land, including gulfweed, which grows along the coast.

On Saturday, the 4th of the same month, a couple of hours before break of day, we had soundings in 110 fathoms, and at nine o'clock we sighted the land. We then drew near to each other, and having put on our gala clothes, we saluted the captain-major by firing our bombards, and dressed the ships with flags and standards.

In the course of the day we tacked so as to come close to the land, but as we failed to identify it, we again stood out to sea.

The Hottentots of St. Helena's Bay

Vasco da Gama struck Africa near St. Helena's Bay, not far from the Cape of Good Hope, a remarkable feat of navigation. He and his weary men had been at sea for ninety-five days—three times as long as Columbus on his discovery of America, and the same amount of time as Magellan on his terrible voyage across the Pacific.

They now found themselves on a barren coast of sand dunes covered by a few parched bushes, almost like the Sahara. From behind the bushes some dark little people peered out at them.

These were the Hottentots, so named by later Dutch settlers because of the stammering, clicking sound of their speech. They were much shorter than the Portuguese, with leathery brown skin, frizzly black hair, and wary eyes. They supported themselves by cattle raising, driving their herds from one skimpy pasturage to another.

When Vasco da Gama had one of them captured and carried on board the *St. Gabriel*, the little fellow's teeth chattered in terror. But when he was released and a boastful sailor named Velloso went among the Hottentots, the small people showed an unexpected fighting spirit, as the *Log-Book* narrates below.

On Tuesday [November 7] we returned to the land, which we found to be low, with a broad bay opening into it. The captain-major sent Pero de Alenquer in a boat to take soundings and to search for good anchoring ground. The bay was found to be very clean, and to afford shelter against all winds except those from the N.W. It extended east and west, and we named it St. Helena.

On Wednesday [November 8] we cast anchor in this bay, and we remained there eight days, cleaning the ships, mending the sails, and taking in wood. . . .

The inhabitants of this country are tawny-colored. Their food is confined to the flesh of seals, whales and gazelles, and the roots of herbs. They are dressed in skins. . . . They are armed with poles of olive wood to which a horn, browned in the fire, is attached. . . .

On . . . Thursday [November 9], we landed with the captain-major, and made captive one of the natives, who was small of stature. . . . This man had been gathering honey in the sandy waste, for in this country the bees deposit their honey at the foot of the mounds around the bushes. He was taken on board the captain-major's ship, and being placed at table he ate of all we ate. On the following day the captain-major had him well dressed and sent ashore.

On the following day [November 10] fourteen or fifteen natives came to where our ships lay. The captain-major landed and showed them a variety of merchandise, with the view of finding out whether such things were to be found in their country. This merchandise included cinnamon, cloves, seed pearls, gold, and many other things, but it was evident that they had no knowledge whatever of such articles, and they were consequently given round bells and tin rings. . . .

On Sunday [November 12] . . . Fernão Velloso . . . expressed a great desire to be permitted to accompany the natives to their houses, so that he might find out how they lived and what they ate. The captain-major . . . allowed him to accompany them, and . . . he went away with the Negroes.

Soon after they had left us they caught a seal, and when they came to the foot of a hill in a barren place they roasted it, and gave some of it to Fernão Velloso, as also some of the roots which they eat. After this meal they expressed a desire that he should not accompany them any further, but return to our vessels. When Fernão Velloso came abreast of the vessels he began to shout, the Negroes keeping in the bush.

We were still at supper; but when his shouts were heard the captain-major rose at once, and so did we others, and we entered a sailing boat. The Negroes then began running along the beach, and they came as quickly up with Fernão Velloso as we did, and when we endeavored to get him into the boat they threw their assegais [spears], and wounded the captain-major and three or four others.

All this happened because we looked upon these people as men of little spirit, quite incapable of violence, and had therefore landed without first arming ourselves. We then returned [with Velloso] to the ships.

Vasco da Gama used the astrolabe and astronomical tables furnished by the king's scholar Zacuto to determine his latitude here. His brother Paul cheerfully took a boatload of seamen whale hunting and harpooned a whale—which dragged their boat half under the waves. They unfastened the harpoon line just in time to escape drowning.

Doubling the Cape

Camoens, in *The Lusiads*, makes the Cape of Good Hope a mythological character named "Adamastor." Adamastor was the son of Earth, a kind of Abominable Snowman who fell desperately in love with a beautiful sea nymph. She tricked him and had him transformed into the rugged Cape at the bottom of the world.

Pero de Alenquer, mentioned in the selection from the *Log-Book* below, was Vasco da Gama's pilot and had been chief pilot ten years earlier under Bartholomew Dias. Vasco placed great reliance on de Alenquer's experience.

At daybreak of Thursday the 16th of November, having careened [overhauled] our ships and taken in wood, we set sail. At that time we did not know how far we might be abaft the Cape of Good Hope.

Pero de Alenquer thought the distance about thirty leagues, but he was not certain, for on his return voyage [with Bartholomew Dias when Dias discovered the Cape] he had left the Cape in the morning and had gone past this bay with the wind astern, whilst on the outward voyage he had kept at sea, and was therefore unable to identify the locality where we now were.

We therefore stood out toward the S.S.W. and late on Saturday [November 18] we beheld the Cape. On that same day we again stood out to sea, returning to the land in the course of the night. On Sunday morning, November 19, we once more made for the Cape, but were again unable to round it, for the wind blew from the S.S.W., whilst the Cape juts out toward the S.W.

We then again stood out to sea, returning to the land on Monday night. At last, on Wednesday [November 22], at noon, having the wind astern, we succeeded in doubling the Cape, and then ran along the coast.

A Dance with the Natives

The bay which the *Log-Book* selection below calls São Bras is today known as Mossel Bay, a beautiful inlet just beyond the Cape. Here Vasco da Gama's men encountered more Hottentots.

The Hottentots loved dancing; their dances sometimes lasted eight days, so they were probably not surprised that while they clapped their hands and danced on shore, even stern Vasco da Gama had music struck up on board the *St. Gabriel* and jigged with his sailors.

It was a great relief to be safely past the "Cape of Storms."

Late on Saturday, November 25, the day of St. Catherine's, we entered the bay of São Bras, where we remained for thirteen days, for there we broke up our storeship and transferred her contents to the other vessels.

On Friday [December 1], whilst still in the bay of São Bras, about ninety men resembling those we had met at St. Helena Bay made their appearance. . . . As soon as we saw them we launched and armed the boats, and started for the land.

When close to the shore the captain-major threw them little round bells, which they picked up. They even ventured to approach us, and took some of these bells from the captain-major's hand. This surprised us greatly, for when Bartholomew Dias was here the natives fled without taking any of the objects which he offered them. . . .

It appeared to us that they did not fly on this occasion, because they had heard from the people at the bay of St. Helena . . . that there was no harm in us, and that we even gave away things which were ours. . . .

On Saturday [December 2] about two hundred Negroes came, both young and old. They brought with them about a dozen oxen and cows and four or five sheep. As soon as we saw them we went ashore. They forthwith began to play on four or five flutes, some producing high notes and others low ones, thus making a pretty harmony for Negroes who are not expected to be musicians; and they danced in the style of Negroes.

The captain-major then ordered the trumpets to be sounded, and we, in the boats, danced, and the captain-major did so likewise. . . .

The next day, Sunday, when the Portuguese landed to refill their casks with badly needed fresh water, the Hottentots became suspicious. Their young warriors crouched in the bush while their leaders asked why the Portuguese "took away their water, and . . . drove their cattle into the bush." Vasco da Gama ordered his landing party to return to the longboats, from which two bombards were fired over the heads of the Hottentots. The natives fled "precipitately."

Whilst taking in water in this bay of São Bras, on a Wednesday, we erected a cross and a pillar. The cross was made out of a mizzenmast, and very high. On the following Thursday [December 7], when about to set sail, we saw about ten or twelve Negroes, who demolished both the cross and the pillar before we had left.

4
Christians and Spices

Scarce on the coast of the strange land were they
When the light barks of fishers they beheld,
Who thereupon before them led the way
To Calicut. . . .

—Luis de Camoens, *The Lusiads*

The Land of the Bantus

"Trade winds" are winds that follow one course across the ocean. (In early English, one meaning of the word *trade* was "direction" or "course.") When these constant winds roll waves against the east coast of a continent, the water strikes the shore and slides off toward the nearer pole. Thus from the east coast of North America the Gulf Stream runs northward. From the east coast of Africa, the Agulhas Current flows strongly southward.

Vasco da Gama's fleet, reduced to the *St. Gabriel,* the *St. Raphael,* and the *Berrio* by the breaking up of the storeship in Mossel Bay, struggled north against this current. On December 16, 1497, the three ships passed the last stone marker (*padrão*) set up by Dias and entered a sea never before explored by Europeans.

A low coast of mangrove forests and swamps, broken by an occasional broad river mouth, moved slowly past their port side. On their right was the endless blue of the Indian Ocean.

Fear of the unknown led some seamen to talk mutiny. But when Vasco da Gama shouted threats of dire punishments, and inflicted a few, the murmurs ceased.

It was the beginning of summer in the southern hemisphere, where the seasons are reversed. As the crews trimmed sails in the balmy air, they remembered legends of the mysterious East—stories of an underground people called "Cave Dwellers," of men who had dogs' heads and barked, and of men who shaded themselves by lying down and holding up a single huge foot. There were stories of the "River of Jewels," of the Biblical land of gold called Ophir, and of Prester John.

On Christmas, 1497, Vasco da Gama named a stretch of coast after the holiday: Natal (the Portuguese word for "Nativity"). On January 11, 1498, he landed for water at a small river where the Negroes were much taller and handsomer than the Hottentots. These Bantu Negroes were friendly and wore many copper ornaments, so the Portuguese named their country the "Land of the Good People" (Terre da Boa Gente) and their river the "Copper River" (Rio do Cobre).

In the selection below, the *Log-Book* describes a settlement of Bantus encountered just beyond the Copper River and the Cape of Currents. Here evidence of Moslem influence, of the Eastern civilization which Vasco da Gama wished to discover, began to appear.

On Monday [January 22, 1498] we discovered a low coast thickly wooded with tall trees. Continuing our course we perceived the broad mouth of a river . . . where . . . we cast anchor. . . .

The country is low and marshy, and covered with tall trees yielding an abundance of various fruits, which the inhabitants eat.

These people are black and well made. They go naked, merely wearing a piece of cotton stuff around their loins, that worn by the women being larger than that worn by the men. The young women are good-looking. Their lips are pierced in three places, and they wear in them bits of twisted tin. These people took much delight in us. They brought us in their *almadias* [dugout canoes] what they had, whilst we went into their village to procure water.

When we had been two or three days at this place two gentlemen of the country came to see us. They were very haughty, and valued nothing which we gave them. One of them wore a *touca* [cap], with a fringe embroidered in silk, and the other a cap of green satin. A young man in their company . . . had come from a distant country, and had already seen big ships like ours.

These tokens [the cap or fez and the knowledge of large ships] gladdened our hearts, for it appeared as if we were really approaching the bourne of our desires. . . .

We spent thirty-two days in the river taking in water, careening the ships, and repairing the mast of the *Raphael.* Many of our men fell ill here, their feet and hands swelling, and their gums growing over their teeth, so that they could not eat.

We erected here a pillar which we called the pillar of St. Raphael, because it had been brought in the ship bearing that name. The river we called Rio dos Bons Signaes (River of Good Signs, or Tokens).

The disease described above was scurvy, now known to be caused by a lack of certain vitamins in the rations. Paul da Gama, Vasco's tenderhearted brother, treated the sick from his own medicine chest, and nursed many back to health.

"Careening" a ship meant overhauling it, cleaning and calking its hull, etc. A ship was floated up on the beach at high tide, anchored, then "careened," or tilted to one side, by having all its cannon shifted to that side. As the tide ebbed, the crew propped timbers under the low side and placed scaffolding on the upper or high side. Then they climbed up the scaffolding to scrape away barnacles, re-place worn planks, and recalk the seams. At the next high tide, the ship was tilted in the opposite direction and its other side cleaned.

Dhows and Coconuts

From the River of Good Signs, Vasco da Gama sailed 330 miles up the coast to Mozambique. He passed between the mainland and the "Island of the Moon" (Madagascar) without sighting this very large island, and he was far out at sea when his ships were opposite Sofala, the southernmost Moslem settlement in East Africa.

Mozambique, on its small coral island, was a port of call for ships going from Sofala north to Kilwa, Mombasa, and Malindi, all trade centers like our East Coast ports of Charleston, Baltimore, New York, and Boston. They contained storehouses, good harbors, neat stone houses, and a mixed population of Arabs, Arab-Bantus, and Bantu natives converted to Mohammedanism. Graceful minarets rose above their other buildings.

Fortunately for the Portuguese, these Moslem cities were like our states under the Articles of Confederation, semi-independent and mutually jealous. Hence they were unable to unite against the Christian intruders. Portuguese ships and cannon overawed their rulers.

The selection from the *Log-Book* below includes descriptions of the Arab dhows, whose planks were not nailed but "sewed" together with coir (rope made from coconut fibers), and of the lofty coconut palm. The Portuguese sailors looked at the hairy brown coconut with its three "eyes" at one end and cried, "*Coco!*" Coco means "goblin" in Portuguese and Spanish; so, from its imagined likeness to a goblin face, the coconut received its name.

On Thursday, the 1st of March [1498], we sighted islands and the mainland, but as it was late we again stood out to sea, and lay to till morning.

We then approached the land . . . and cast anchor at a distance of two bowshots from the village [of Mozambique].

The people of this country are of a ruddy complexion and well made. They are Mohammedans, and their language is the same as that of the Moors. Their dresses are of fine linen or cotton stuffs, with variously colored stripes, and of rich and elaborate workmanship. They all wear *toucas* with borders of silk embroidered in gold.

They are merchants, and have transactions with white Moors, four of whose vessels were at the time in port, laden with gold, silver, cloves, pepper, ginger, and silver rings, as also with quantities of pearls, jewels, and rubies, all of which articles are used by the people of this country.

We understood them to say that all these things, with the exception of the gold, were brought thither by these Moors; that further on, where we were going to, they abounded, and that precious stones, pearls, and spices were so plentiful that there was no need to purchase them as they could be collected in baskets. . . .

We were told, morever, that Prester John resided not far from this place; that he held many cities along the coast, and that the inhabitants of those cities were great merchants and owned big ships. The residence of Prester John was said to be far in the interior, and

could be reached only on the back of camels. . . .
This information . . . rendered us so happy that we
cried with joy. . . .

The vessels of this country are of good size and
decked. There are no nails, and the planks are held
together by cords [coir ropes], as are also those of
their boats. The sails are made of palm matting. Their
mariners have Genoese needles [compasses], by which
they steer, quadrants, and navigating charts.

The flimsy Arab dhows could not carry guns because at
the recoil of a cannon being fired a dhow literally came
apart at the seams, the ropes breaking and the ship disinte-
grating. One fanciful explanation of why the Arabs did
not use nails was that in the Indian Ocean near Ceylon
there was thought to be a giant loadstone, or magnetic
mountain, which would draw all the nails out of passing
ships.

The palms of this country yield a fruit as large as
a melon, of which the kernel is eaten. It has a nutty
flavor. There also grow in abundance melons and cu-
cumbers, which were brought to us for barter. . . .

The Lord of the place . . . took us for Turks or
for Moors from some foreign land, for in case we
came from Turkey he begged to be shown the bows of
our country and our books of the Law. But when
they learned that we were Christians they arranged
to seize and kill us by treachery. . . .

After leaving Mozambique once and being forced back

by opposing currents, Vasco da Gama took a party to the "watering place" of Mozambique, which was on the mainland. When he had to drive off a band of Moors to obtain water, he was furious. The next day he determined to teach the Moors a lesson.

On Sunday morning, the 24th of March . . . a Moor came abreast of our ships, and sneeringly told us that if we wanted water we might go in search of it, giving us to understand that we should meet with something which would make us turn back. The captain-major no sooner heard this threat than he resolved to go, in order to show that we were able to do them harm if we desired it.

We forthwith armed our boats, placing bombards in their poops, and started for the . . . town.

The Moors had constructed palisades by lashing planks together, so that those behind them could not be seen. They were at the time walking along the beach, armed with assegais, swords, bows, and slings, with which they hurled stones at us. But our bombards soon made it so hot for them that they fled behind their palisades; but this turned out to their injury rather than their profit.

During the three hours that we were occupied in this manner, bombarding the town, we saw two men killed, one on the beach and the other behind the palisades. When we were weary of this work we retired to our ships to dine.

A Treacherous Attack

Vasco da Gama now sailed north, just outside the stepping-stone coral islands, with two pilots from Mozambique who later proved untrustworthy. On April 7, 1498, lookouts sighted a high, sandy island crowned with houses—Mombasa. Vasco da Gama stared suspiciously at the Moslem town and had his three ships anchor just beyond the harbor.

Mombasa, like Mozambique, was only a short distance from the mainland. Its port, the best in East Africa, was crowded with dhows laden with such luxury goods as stoneware from Siam and Canton porcelain from China, for which the Mombasa merchants traded ivory, gold, slaves, and iron ore which was made into steel blades for Indian swords and daggers.

Many of Vasco da Gama's men were still ill with scurvy. They looked across the water at the whitewashed houses gleaming in the tropical sunshine and murmured wistfully, "It is like Portugal!"

But Vasco himself had no leisure for homesickness. The Moors now understood that he and his men were Christians. Suppose news of the bombardment of Mozambique had arrived here ahead of his high black ships?

"Break out all flags!" he ordered briskly. "Only able-bodied men remain on deck. All others below!"

He would make an impressive, gala entry and hope for the best. But starting at midnight, as the *Log-Book* relates, his fears were to be confirmed.

On Saturday [April 7, 1498] we cast anchor off Mombasa, but did not enter the port. No sooner had we been perceived than a [dhow] manned by Moors came out to us: in front of the city there lay numerous vessels all dressed in flags. And we, anxious not to be outdone, also dressed our ships, and we actually surpassed their show, for we wanted in nothing but men, even the few whom we had being very ill. . . .

The pilots who had come with us told us there resided both Moors and Christians in this city; that these latter lived apart under their own lords, and that on our arrival they would receive us with much honor and take us to their houses. But they said this for a purpose of their own, for it was not true.

At midnight there approached us a [dhow] with about a hundred men, all armed with cutlasses and bucklers. When they came to the vessel of the captain-major [the *St. Gabriel*] they attempted to board her, armed as they were, but this was not permitted, only four or five of the most distinguished men among them being allowed on board. They remained about a couple of hours, and it seemed to us that they paid us this visit merely to find out whether they might not capture one or the other of our vessels. . . .

On Tuesday [April 10], when weighing anchor to enter the port, the captain-major's vessel would not pay off, and struck the vessel which followed astern. We therefore again cast anchor. When the Moors who were in our ship saw that we did not go on, they scrambled into a [dhow] attached to our stern; whilst the two pilots whom we had brought from Mozambique jumped into the water, and were picked up by the men in the [dhow].

At night the captain-major "questioned" [tortured] two Moors from Mozambique whom we had on board, by dropping boiling oil upon their skin, so that they might confess any treachery intended against us. They said that orders had been given to capture us as soon as we entered the port, and thus to avenge what we had done at Mozambique. And when this torture was being applied a second time, one of the Moors, although his hands were tied, threw himself into the sea, whilst the other did so during the morning watch. [Both swam ashore.]

About midnight two *almadias* [dugout canoes], with many men in them, approached. The *almadias* stood off whilst the men entered the water, some swimming in the direction of the *Berrio*, others in that of the *Raphael*. Those who swam to the *Berrio* began to cut the cable.

The men on watch thought at first that they were tunny [tuna] fish, but when they perceived their mistake they shouted to the other vessels. The other swimmers had already got hold of the rigging of the mizzenmast. Seeing themselves discovered, they silently slipped down and fled. These and other wicked tricks were practiced upon us by these dogs, but our Lord did not allow them to succeed, because they were unbelievers. . . .

It pleased God in his mercy that on arriving at this

city all our sick recovered their health, for the climate
of this place is very good.

Malindi: Gateway to India

From Mombasa, Vasco da Gama had only a two-day sail
north to Malindi, where at last he found friends. Malindi
("Deep Channel") was on the mainland, the northernmost
town the Portuguese visited in the chain of Arab trading
centers which extended south to the Cape of Currents. Its
aged king was feuding with Mombasa.

On the voyage to Malindi, Vasco da Gama, seeking
pilots to guide him to India, captured the crew of a dhow
and its two passengers—an old Arab and his young wife.
When he arrived opposite the town, Vasco set the old
Arab ashore on a sandbank to negotiate with the ruler.

Vasco da Gama was very cautious here, insisting that
any interview with Malindian officials take place out in
the harbor. Two days later he climbed into a longboat; the
son of the king came out in a dhow, and the two shouted
questions and answers across the waves. While the beauti-
fully carved Moorish *anafils* (trumpets of ivory and
wood) emitted what Camoens called a "hellish roar,"
Vasco da Gama began a friendship between Portugal and
Malindi that was to last for a century. Even Vasco's im-
patience was curbed for a few days, until the pilots promised by the king failed to appear.

Meanwhile, as the *Log-Book* narrates below, his men
found people whom they mistook for the Christians they
had been seeking.

[April 14] at sunset, we cast anchor off a place
called Malindi, which is thirty leagues from Mombasa. . . .

On Wednesday [April 18] . . . when the [son of the] king came up close to the ships in a [dhow], the captain-major at once entered one of his boats . . . and many friendly words were exchanged when they lay side by side. The [son of the] king having invited the captain-major to come to his house to rest . . . the captain-major said that he was not permitted by his master [King Manuel of Portugal] to go on land. . . .

When both had said all they desired, the captain-major sent for the Moors whom he had taken prisoner, and surrendered them all. This gave much satisfaction to the [son of the] king. . . .

We found here four vessels belonging to Indian Christians. When they came for the first time on board Paul da Gama's ship [the *St. Raphael*], the captain-major being there at the time, they were shown an altarpiece representing Our Lady at the foot of the cross, with Jesus Christ in her arms and the apostles around her. When the Indians saw this picture they prostrated themselves, and as long as we were there they came to say their prayers in front of it. . . . They told us that they ate no beef. . . .

Actually these Indians were Hindus. The Hindu religion resembles the ancient Greek in having many gods who are represented in statues and pictures. The Hindus mistook the figures of the Christian saints for figures of their gods. They did not eat beef because the cow is sacred in the Hindu religion.

On the following Sunday, the 22nd of April, the king's [dhow] brought on board one of his confidential servants, and as two days had passed without any visitors, the captain-major had this man seized, and sent word to the king that he required the pilots whom he had promised. The king, when he received this message, sent a Christian pilot, and the captain-major allowed the gentleman, whom he had retained in his vessel, to go away.

We were much pleased with the Christian pilot whom the king had sent us. . . .

The town of Malindi lies in a bay and extends along the shore. It may be likened to Alcochete [a Portuguese town near Lisbon]. Its houses are lofty and well whitewashed, and have many windows; on the landside are palm groves, and all around it maize and vegetables are being cultivated.

We remained in front of this town during nine days, and all this time we had fêtes, sham fights, and musical performances ("fanfares").

The Southwest Monsoon

On April 24, 1498, Vasco da Gama bade farewell to Malindi and Africa. Their friendly hosts had entertained the Portuguese with a fireworks display. Now the ships stood out of the harbor in line, and their new pilot, the impassive Ahmad ibn Majid, was stationed beside Vasco on the poop of the *St. Gabriel*. The southwest monsoon sped them toward India.

A monsoon (Arabic *mausim*—"season") is a seasonal wind caused by the difference in temperature between air over land and air over sea. Cool air is heavier, exerts greater pressure, than warm air. Cool air (from a "high pressure" area) will flow toward warm air (in a "low pressure" area). Thus if the land is cooler than the sea, a "land breeze" blows from the land toward the sea. If the sea is cooler than the land, a "sea breeze" blows from the sea toward the land.

When the earth's temperature is falling, the land cools more rapidly than the sea. From November to March the land breeze blows from the cool, high pressure area over Asia toward the Indian Ocean and the African coast. This is the winter (northeast) monsoon.

When the earth's temperature is rising, the land heats up more rapidly than the sea. From April to September the sea breeze blows from the cool, high pressure area over the Indian Ocean toward India and the Asian continent. This is the summer (southwest) monsoon, on which for centuries the farmers of India have depended for their rain. A "bad monsoon," bringing less rain than usual, means famine.

Vasco da Gama's fleet must have been propelled by a "good monsoon." And Vasco da Gama was also helped by the expert piloting of Ahmad ibn Majid, according to one contemporary "the most trustworthy of the many pilots . . . of the west coast of India." Ahmad was a Moslem whose green turban showed that he had made the pilgrimage to Mecca. But if the Portuguese mistakenly wished to consider him an Indian "Christian," Ahmad apparently didn't mind.

For three weeks, as the *Log-Book* narrates below, he guided the fleet across the Indian Ocean without mishap. On the twenty-fifth and twenty-sixth days they sighted high land through a curtain of monsoon rain. On the twenty-seventh day Ahmad identified these hills as the Western Ghats, near Calicut.

The Portuguese had reached India.

We left Malindi on Tuesday, the 24th of the month [of April] for a city called Calicut, with the pilot whom the king had given us. The coast there runs north and south, and the land encloses a huge bay with a strait. In this bay [the Arabian Sea], we were told, were to be found many large cities of Christians and Moors, including one called Cambay, as also six hundred known islands, and within it the Red Sea and the "house" of Mecca.

On the following Sunday [April 29] we once more saw the North Star, which we had not seen for a long time.

On Friday, the 18th of May, after having seen no land for twenty-three days, we sighted lofty mountains, and having all this time sailed before the wind we could not have made less than six hundred leagues. The land, when first sighted, was at a distance of eight leagues, and our lead reached bottom at forty-five fathoms. That same night we took a course to the S.S.W., so as to get away from the coast.

On the following day [May 19] we again approached the land, but owing to the heavy rain and a thunderstorm, which prevailed whilst we were sailing along the coast, our pilot was unable to identify the exact locality. On Sunday [May 20] we found ourselves close to some mountains, and when we were near enough for the pilot to recognize them he told us that they were above Calicut, and that this was the country we desired to go to.

Arrival at Calicut

Calicut lies on the southwestern side—on the Malabar Coast—of India. India is shaped like an upside-down isosceles triangle. Its base in the north consists of the mighty double wall of the Himalayas ("snow abodes"), for centuries a barrier against invaders. Below the Himalayas is the wide river plain, watered by three streams fed by the melted snow of the mountains: the Indus, the Ganges, and the Brahmaputra. This is the more fertile and thickly populated half of India.

South India, where Vasco da Gama landed, is cut off from the north by the Vindhya Mountains, which run horizontally across the Indian triangle below the river plain. South India is a high plateau which ends at both east and west coasts in a series of peaks called *ghats* ("landing stairs"), precipices rising out of the sea or looming just behind the narrow coastal strip. Its people are of Dravidian stock, the darker, earlier inhabitants of India, contrasting with the lighter-skinned Aryans who ages ago invaded India from Afghanistan and settled in the northern river plain.

Along the Malabar ("hill country") Coast of South India, the Portuguese found semi-independent cities with Indian rulers but also with colonies of Arab traders upon whose business the Indians depended for their prosperity. Names of cities such as Goa, Cananore, Cochin, and Calicut—the most important of all—would soon become household words in Portugal. But to the seamen who furled their sails in the open roadstead, all was new and strange.

The Portuguese stared out across the water at nearby fishing communities of reed-covered huts and small boats, at graceful coconut palms and the confusion of temples, palaces, adobe houses, mosques and markets which was Calicut.

When they entered the city, they were overwhelmed by the sounds and sights of the East. Swarms of brown men wearing white loin cloths and turbans, of women in bright saris with jangling bracelets on their arms, filled the narrow streets, along with squawking chickens, dogs, and gaunt cows, which were not to be harmed because they were sacred.

Monkeys swung from palm trees; parakeets screeched from palm-thatched roofs. In doorways and arches, beggars thrust out skeletonlike hands, or slept, squatting, like battle-worn soldiers. Urchins screamed insults as they darted among the crowds. Ox carts with solid wooden wheels creaked patiently along.

The *Log-Book* selection below gives a good description of the trade in spices which enriched Calicut. Silk from China, cloves and nutmeg from the Spice Islands (Indonesia) were brought to Calicut and there transshipped to Egypt, all in Mecca vessels—one-masted Arab ships which crowded the roadstead. In addition, Calicut offered its own famous cotton cloth called "calico" (from "Calicut"); black pepper grown on vines along the hillsides behind the city; also cinnamon, ginger, and jewels. Boxes and bales were piled in warehouses by the sea, and goods were displayed in shops protected from the hot sun by awnings.

Vasco da Gama's eyes gleamed at the sight of this fabulous wealth.

That night [May 20] we anchored two leagues from the city of Calicut . . . about a league and a

half from the shore. After we were at anchor, four boats approached us from the land, who asked of what nation we were. We told them, and they then pointed out Calicut to us.

On the following day [May 21] these same boats came again alongside, when the captain-major sent one of the convicts to Calicut, and those with whom he went took him to two Moors from Tunis, who could speak Castilian and Genoese. The first greeting that he received was in these words:

"May the Devil take thee! What brought you hither?"

They asked what he sought so far away from home, and he told them that we came in search of Christians and of spices.

They said: "Why does not the King of Castile, the King of France, or the Signoria of Venice send hither?"

He said that the King of Portugal would not consent to their doing so, and they [the two Moors] said he [the King of Portugal] did the right thing. After this conversation they took him to their lodgings and gave him wheaten bread and honey.

When he had eaten he returned to the ships, accompanied by one of the Moors, who was no sooner on board than he said these words:

"A lucky venture, a lucky venture! Plenty of rubies, plenty of emeralds! You owe great thanks to

God, for having brought you to a country holding
such riches!"

We were greatly astonished to hear his talk, for we
never expected to hear our language spoken so far
away from Portugal.

One of the Moors who astounded the Portuguese by
hailing them in Spanish was a native of North Africa who
had once done business with the Portuguese in the Mediterranean. His name was Monçaide. Later Monçaide
warned the Portuguese of Moslem plots against them, and
had to flee for his life from the Moslems of Calicut. Vasco
da Gama carried him back to Portugal.

The convict mentioned above was one of the ten or
twelve sent with da Gama for employment on especially
dangerous tasks. Portuguese explorers often carried convicts to be used in this way.

The city of Calicut is inhabited by Christians
[really, Hindus]. They are of a tawny complexion.
Some of them have big beards and long hair, whilst
others clip their hair short or shave the head, merely
allowing a tuft to remain on the crown. . . . They
also wear mustaches. They pierce the ears and wear
much gold in them. They go naked down to the
waist, covering their lower extremities with very fine
cotton stuffs. But it is only the most respectable who
do this, for the others manage as best they are able.

The women of this country, as a rule, are ugly and
of small stature. They wear many jewels of gold
round the neck, numerous bracelets on their arms,

and rings set with precious stones on their toes. All these people are well-disposed and apparently of mild temper. At first sight they seem covetous and ignorant. . . .

From this country of Calicut . . . come the spices which are consumed in the East and the West, in Portugal, as in all other countries of the world, as also precious stones of every description. The following spices are to be found in this city of Calicut, being its own produce: much ginger and pepper and cinnamon. . . . Cloves are brought to this city from an island called Malacca.

The Mecca vessels carry these spices from there to . . . Jidda. . . . The merchandise is then transshipped to smaller vessels, which carry it through the Red Sea to a place close to St. Catherine of Mount Sinai. . . . From that place the merchants carry the spices on the back of camels . . . to Cairo. . . . On this road to Cairo they are frequently robbed by thieves . . . such as the Bedouins. . . .

At Cairo the spices are embarked on the river Nile, which rises in Prester John's country . . . and descending that river for two days they reach a place called Rosetta. . . . There they are placed on camels, and are conveyed in one day to a city called Alexandria, which is a seaport. This city is visited by the galleys of Venice and Genoa, in search of these spices, which yield the Grand Sultan a revenue of

600,000 cruzados [over $3,000,000] in customs duties.

In a "Christian Church"

One of the first places the Portuguese visited in Calicut was a "church," which turned out to have some strange furnishings. The *Log-Book* describes the visit below.

When we arrived at Calicut they took us to a large church, and this is what we saw:

The body of the church is as large as a monastery, all built of hewn stone and covered with tiles. At the main entrance rises a pillar of bronze as high as a mast, on the top of which was perched a bird, apparently a cock. In addition to this, there was another pillar as high as a man, and very stout.

In the center of the body of the church rose a chapel, all built of hewn stone, with a bronze door sufficiently wide for a man to pass, and stone steps leading up to it. Within this sanctuary stood a small image which they said represented Our Lady. Along the walls, by the main entrance, hung seven small bells. In this church the captain-major said his prayers, and we with him.

We did not go within the chapel, for it is the custom that only certain servants of the church, called *quafees* [Brahman priests], should enter. These *quafees* wore some threads passing over the left shoulder and under the right arm, in the same manner as our deacons wear the stole.

They threw holy water over us, and gave us some white earth, which the Christians of this country are in the habit of putting on their foreheads, breasts, around the neck, and on the forearms. They threw holy water upon the captain-major and gave him some of the earth, which he gave in charge of someone, giving them to understand that he would put it on later.

Many . . . saints were painted on the walls of the church, wearing crowns. They were painted variously, with teeth protruding an inch from the mouth, and four or five arms.

Although there are today several ancient Christian communities in India with a tradition that St. Thomas landed on the Malabar Coast around A.D. 46 and founded seven churches there, the "church" described above was almost certainly a Hindu temple. At this time the "St. Thomas Christians" were found farther south, in Cranganore (near Cochin), not in Calicut. The Portuguese mistook the Hindus for badly instructed Christians, and Europe at first believed their account of "Christian" Calicut.

Actually the "seven small bells" mentioned above were the bells struck by the Brahmans (the priestly caste) as they entered the temple. The pictures of "saints" with four or five arms were representations of Hindu gods such as Vishnu and Siva; the extra arms symbolized their divine power. The image of "Our Lady" may have been a statue of Gauri, the Hindu "White Goddess," or of another goddess named Mari.

A few of the Portuguese did have doubts about this "church." John da Sá, Vasco da Gama's clerk, muttered as he knelt beside his taciturn commander: "If these be devils, I worship the true God!"

A Message for the Zamorin

Accompanied by thirteen of his seamen, Vasco da Gama was now carried in a litter to the tree-shaded palace of the ruler of Calicut, the Zamorin. In the palace, Nairs—small, wiry warriors with swords in red leather sheaths—escorted the Portuguese through rose-scented chambers to the throne room.

The amiable Zamorin ("Lord of the Sea"), clad in a silk garment from his waist down, with gold bracelets and jewels on his arms and ankles, seemed well disposed toward Vasco da Gama. It was to his interest to welcome traders to Calicut. At the same time he was aware that the Arabs, to whom he was indebted, were hostile toward da Gama.

The *Log-Book* below describes Vasco da Gama's interview with the Zamorin.

After we had left that place [the "church"] . . . the crowd grew so dense that progress along the street became next to impossible. . . .

The king [Zamorin] sent a brother of the *bale* [chief of police], who was a lord of this country, to accompany the captain, and he was attended by men beating drums, blowing *anafils* [trumpets] and bagpipes, and firing off matchlocks. . . . The . . . people . . . surrounded us, and . . . crowded the roofs and houses. . . .

It was then an hour before sunset. When we reached the palace we passed through a gate into a courtyard of great size, and before we arrived at where the king was, we passed four doors, through which we had to force our way, giving many blows to the people. . . .

The king was in a small court, reclining upon a couch covered with a cloth of green velvet. . . . In his left hand the king held a very large golden cup [spittoon], having a capacity of eight pints. . . . Into this cup the king threw the husks of a certain herb [betel nut] which is chewed by the people of this country because of its soothing effects. . . . The canopy above the couch was all gilt.

The captain, on entering, saluted in the manner of the country: by putting the hands together, then raising them toward Heaven, as is done by Christians when addressing God, and immediately afterward opening them and shutting the fists quickly. The king beckoned to the captain with his right hand to come nearer. . . .

The captain-major [said] that he was the ambassador of the King of Portugal, and the bearer of a message which he could only deliver to him personally.

The king said this was good, and immediately asked him [da Gama] to be conducted to a chamber. . . . [In the chamber] the king . . . threw himself upon another couch, covered with various stuffs embroidered in gold, and asked the captain what he wanted.

And the captain told him he was the ambassador

of a King of Portugal, who was Lord of many countries and the possessor of great wealth. . . . [The King of Portugal] had ordered him to build three vessels, of which he had been appointed captain-major, and . . . had ordered him not to return to Portugal until he should have discovered this King of the Christians [the Zamorin]. . . . Two letters had been intrusted to him [Vasco da Gama] to be presented . . . and . . . he would do so on the ensuing day; and, finally, he had been instructed to say . . . that he [the King of Portugal] desired to be his friend and brother.

In reply to this the king said that he was welcome; that, on his part, he held him as a friend and brother. . . . These and many other things passed between the two in this chamber, and as it was already late in the night . . . the captain took leave of the king and came to where we were, that is, to a veranda lit up by a huge candlestick. By that time four hours of the night had already gone.

We then all went forth with the captain in search of our lodgings, and a countless crowd with us. And the rain poured down so heavily that the streets ran with water.

Vasco da Gama was satisfied with his reception by the bland, hospitable Zamorin. As the days passed, he was to discover another aspect of the Indian character, a genius for delay and evasion, but tonight the Portuguese were optimistic.

The dangers of the voyage were behind them. They had carried the white silken banner of the Knights of Christ, blazoned with the red cross, all the way from Portugal around Africa, and planted it before Calicut.

What could they now win, for their faith and themselves, in the golden East?

5
"Portugal! Portugal!"

Gama considered in himself likewise
The time had come which told him to depart . . .
From a king who cherished Moslems in his heart.

—Luis de Camoens, *The Lusiads*

Gifts Unfit for a King

Fortunately for the Portuguese, the great Hindu kingdom of Vijayanagar, which included most of South India and to which the Zamorin was nominally subject, was locked in a death struggle with Moslem foes to the north. At first neither Vijayanagar ("Victory City") nor the Zamorin considered the Portuguese as anything but troublesome pirates. Calicut's Arab merchants knew better but misinformed the Zamorin.

Vasco da Gama, however, expected the Zamorin to respect him as the ambassador of Christian Europe; to rally the "Christians" of Calicut to da Gama's side; and to oppose the Arab merchants. He was knocking at the gates of the East, but Vasco by nature knocked haughtily, and hard enough to irritate his hosts.

He did attempt to gain the Zamorin's favor by bringing him presents. Eastern merchants gave this luxury-loving ruler gold and precious stones. Vasco da Gama offered him pieces of cloth, caps, strings of beads, some oil and honey, and a few washbasins—trinkets you could pick up today in a ten-cent store!

As the *Log-Book* relates below, the Zamorin was not impressed with Vasco da Gama's gifts.

On Tuesday [May 29, 1498] the captain got ready the following things to be sent to the king, viz., twelve pieces of lambel [striped cloth], four scarlet hoods, six hats, four strings of coral, a case containing six wash-hand basins, a case of sugar, two casks of oil, and two of honey. And as it is the custom not to send anything to the king without the knowledge of the Moor, his factor [agent], and of the *bale* [chief of police], the captain informed them of his intention.

They came, and when they saw the present they laughed at it, saying that it was not a thing to offer to a king, that the poorest merchant from Mecca, or any other part of India, gave more, and that if he wanted to make a present it should be in gold, as the king would not accept such things.

When the captain heard this he grew sad, and said that he had brought no gold, that, moreover, he was no merchant, but an ambassador. . . .

On Wednesday morning the Moors returned, and took the captain to the palace, and us others with him. The palace was crowded with armed men. Our captain was kept waiting with his conductors for fully four long hours, outside a door, which was only opened when the king sent word to admit him. ΄. . .

When he had entered, the king said . . . that he had told him that he came from a very rich kingdom, and yet had brought him nothing; that he had also told him that he was the bearer of a letter, which had not yet been delivered.

To this the captain rejoined that he had brought nothing, because the object of his voyage was merely to make discoveries, but that when other ships came he would then see what they brought him; as to the letter, it was true that he had brought one, and would deliver it immediately.

The king then asked what it was he had come to discover: stones or men? If he came to discover men, as he said, why had he brought nothing? Moreover, he had been told that he carried with him the golden image of a Santa Maria. The captain said that the Santa Maria was not of gold, and that even if she were he would not part with her, as she had guided him across the ocean, and would guide him back to his own country.

The king then asked for the letter. . . . Four Moors took the letter and read it between them, after which they translated it to the king, who was well satisfied with its contents.

The king then asked what kind of merchandise was to be found in his [da Gama's] country. The captain said there was much corn, cloth, iron, bronze, and many other things. The king asked whether he had any merchandise with him. The captain replied that he had a little of each sort, as samples. . . . The king said . . . he might . . . land his merchandise, and sell it to the best advantage. Having taken leave of the king the captain returned to his lodgings, and we with him.

Under Arrest

The Zamorin was urged by Arab traders to drive the Portuguese away, but hesitated. According to one sixteenth century historian (Corrêa), Vasco da Gama boasted that his three ships were only part of a fleet of fifty on the way to India. If Vasco made this statement, and if the Zamorin believed him, the Zamorin would not have wanted to offend the Portuguese. At this time he had no more than two cannon with which to defend Calicut.

The Portuguese seamen danced and sang in the streets to the sound of Indian trumpets (*anafils*), or watched elephants push a ship up on shore from the sea with their heads, while the Zamorin temporized. Then, on his way back to the ships from his second interview with the Zamorin, Vasco da Gama and his escort were temporarily arrested.

The Arabs may have bribed Indian officials to act thus in the hope of provoking Vasco da Gama into a violent reaction. On the other hand, the Zamorin, caught between the two sides, may have ordered the Portuguese guarded to protect them from Arab assassins. In either case, Vasco da Gama's bold demands led to increased tension and a setback.

The selection below is from the *Log-Book*.

[The next day] the captain [Vasco da Gama] started at once for Pandarani [fourteen miles north of Calicut], where our ships were, many people following him. We others, not being able to keep up with him, were left behind. Trudging thus along we were overtaken by the *bale,* who passed on to join the captain. We lost our way, and wandered far inland, but the *bale* sent a man after us, who put us on the right road.

When we reached Pandarani we found the captain inside a rest house, of which there were many along the road, so that travelers and wayfarers might find protection against the rain.

The *bale* and many others were with the captain. On our arrival the captain asked the *bale* for a

[boat], so that we might go to our ships; but the *bale* and the others said that it was already late—in fact, the sun had set—and that he should go next day. . . .

[The next morning, June 1] the captain again asked for boats to take him to his ships. They then began to whisper among themselves, and said that we should have them if we would order our vessels to come nearer the shore.

Pandarani, where the Zamorin had ordered da Gama's fleet to anchor, was a much safer berth than Calicut; but da Gama, suspicious of Indian and Moslem alike, refused to station his ships close to the shore. In stormy weather it was dangerous for the *bale*'s men to have to row da Gama so far out to his ship.

The captain said that if he ordered his vessels to approach his brother would think that he was being held a prisoner, and that he gave this order on compulsion, and would hoist the sails and return to Portugal.

They said that if we refused to order the ships to come nearer we should not be permitted to embark . . . [and] they immediately closed all the doors, and many armed men entered to guard us. . . .

They then asked us to give up our sails and rudders. The captain declared that he would give up none of these things. . . .

The captain and we others felt very downhearted,

though outwardly we pretended not to notice what they did. The captain said that . . . his men . . . would die of hunger. But they said that we must remain where we were, and that if we died of hunger . . . they cared nothing for that. . . .

The captain did not wish the ships to come within the port, for it seemed to him—as it did to us—that once inside they could easily be captured, after which they would first kill him, and then us others, as we were already in their power.

We passed all that day most anxiously. At night more people surrounded us . . . and we were no longer allowed to walk in the compound . . . but confined within a small tiled court, with a multitude of people around us. . . .

On the following day, Saturday, June 2, in the morning, these gentlemen [the *bale* and others] came back, and this time they "wore better faces." They told the captain that as he had informed the king that he intended to land his merchandise, he should now give orders to have this done. . . .

The captain consented, and said he would write to his brother to see to its being done. They said this was well, and that immediately after the arrival of the merchandise he would be permitted to return to his ship. The captain at once wrote to his brother to send him certain things. . . . On their receipt the captain was allowed to go on board, two men remaining behind with the things that had been landed.

At this we rejoiced greatly . . . for we knew well that once the captain was on board those who had been landed would have nothing to fear. When the captain reached his ship he ordered that no more merchandise should be sent.

The guards around Vasco da Gama and his men carried swords and glittering, lacquered shields, and wore caps and coats padded with cotton. Fighting an Indian soldier of this period was like fighting a pillow. Little brass rings on their swords clinked cheerfully during a duel.

Battles were conducted with great ceremony. Night attacks and ambushes were banned as unsportsmanlike. The armies faced each other on a wide plain like opposing football teams. No blow could be struck until a trumpet which required four men to lift was sounded and drums beat on both sides. Numerous scribes were present to take notes for a play-by-play account of the fighting. The only aim was to capture the enemy's camp, and after one battle both armies disbanded and went home. Brahman priests had established these rules to make war less savage.

The Malice of the Moors

The Moslem population of Calicut included not only the prosperous, aggressive Arab traders but also the fanatical "Moplahs," descendants of Arabs who had come to Calicut centuries earlier and married Indian women. The Moplahs were zealous Mohammedans and notorious troublemakers. Both they and the traders showed their hatred for Vasco da Gama's men when the groups passed each other in the streets.

Meanwhile the most influential Arab merchants badgered the Zamorin as follows:

"Most renowned Prince . . . have not the Portuguese

. . . made themselves masters of most of the towns of Africa? . . . They have fallen upon Mozambique . . . [and] made great slaughter at Mombasa. . . . If with so small a force they dare show the ferocity of their disposition, what will they not perpetrate when they have greater strength? If you have any regard for the welfare of your kingdom, destroy these pernicious wretches!"

The *Log-Book* narrates the continuing conflict below.

Five days afterward [on June 7] the captain sent word to the king that, although he had sent him straight back to his ships, certain of his people had detained him a night and a day on the road; that he had landed his merchandise as he had been ordered, but that the Moors only came to depreciate it; and that for these reasons he looked forward to what he (the king) would order; that he placed no value upon this merchandise, but that he and his ships were at his service.

The king at once sent word saying that those who acted thus were bad [men], and that he would punish them. He, at the same time, sent seven or eight merchants to inspect the merchandise, and to become purchasers if they felt inclined. He also sent a man of quality to remain with the factor already there, and authorized them to kill any Moor who might go there, without fear of punishment.

The merchants whom the king had sent remained about eight days, but instead of buying they depreciated the merchandise. The Moors no longer visited the house where the merchandise was, but they bore us no good will, and when one of us landed they spat on the ground, saying: "Portugal! Portugal!" Indeed from the very first they had sought means to take and kill us.

When the captain found that the merchandise found no buyers at that place [Pandarani], he applied to the king for permission to forward it to Calicut. The king at once ordered the *bale* to get a sufficient number of men who were to carry the whole on their backs to Calicut, this to be done at his expense. . . .

But all this was done because it was intended to do us some ill turn, for it had been reported to the king that we were thieves and went about to steal.

Indian Visitors

The Zamorin had the Portuguese merchandise transferred to Calicut on June 24, 1498, but shoppers still looked, spat, and walked away without buying. Vasco da Gama frowned, but tried to improve relations with the Indians by permitting curious citizens to visit his ships, and by sharing his food with them. Although there was much wealth in Calicut, many of its common people were hungry.

Many of these visitors were of low caste, the group which later Portuguese writers called "Poleas" (pariahs). *Caste* itself is a Portuguese word, meaning "lineage." The Indian word for caste is *varna*, which means "color"—indicating that in the beginning India's elaborate caste system was based on color prejudice. The lighter Aryan invaders considered themselves superior to the darker native Dravidians.

Originally there were four castes: the white-garmented,

dignified Brahmans (the priestly caste); the Kshatriya (the warrior caste); the competent Vaishya (the commercial caste); and the ragged Sudra (the servant caste). By the fifteenth century these four castes had been subdivided into many others. Each Indian was supposed to marry within the caste he was born into, to follow its occupation, and to observe its elaborate rules about eating and drinking.

The selection below is from the *Log-Book*.

On Sunday, the 24th of June, being the day of St. John the Baptist, the merchandise left for Calicut. The captain then ordered that all our people should visit that town by turns, and in the following manner: Each ship was to send a man ashore, on whose return another should be sent. In this way all would have their turn, and would be able to make such purchases as they desired.

These men were made welcome by the Christians [really, Hindus] along the road, who showed much pleasure when one of them entered a house, to eat or to sleep, and they gave them freely of all they had.

At the same time many men came on board our ships to sell us fish in exchange for bread, and they were made welcome by us. Many of them were accompanied by their sons and little children, and the captain ordered that they should be fed. All this was done for the sake of establishing relations of peace and amity, and to induce them to speak well of us and not evil.

So great was the number of these visitors that

sometimes it was night before we could get rid of them; and this was due to the dense population of the country and the scarcity of food. It even happened that when some of our men were engaged in mending a sail, and took biscuits with them to eat, that old and young fell upon them, took the biscuits out of their hands, and left them nothing to eat. . . .

All on board ship went on land by twos and threes, taking with them bracelets, clothes, new shirts, and other articles, which they desired to sell. We did not, however, effect these sales at the prices hoped for . . . [but] sold . . . cheaply . . . in order to take some things away from this country, if only for samples. Those who visited the city bought there cloves, cinnamon, and precious stones; and having bought what they desired they came back to the ships. . . .

When the captain found the people of the country so well disposed, he left a factor with the merchandise [on shore], together with a clerk and some other men.

Departure from Calicut

August on the Malabar Coast. Thunderheads piled up over the Western Ghats. Sudden downpours turned dirt streets into quagmires, caused water to run in sheets from the eaves of Hindu temples, and blotted out Calicut for the ships anchored in the roadstead. India was a green but steaming earth.

Two months had passed. The Indian visitors still came to the *St. Gabriel, St. Raphael,* and *Berrio,* but there was "No Sale" for the Portuguese goods; so Vasco da Gama decided to return to Lisbon. He was annoyed with his fellow "Christians" of Calicut. When he informed the Zamorin of his wish to depart, however, the Zamorin gave him reason to become furious.

A large sum in customs charges must first be paid, said the Zamorin; and to make sure that they were paid, the Zamorin arrested Diogo Dias (brother of Bartholomew Dias) and his men, who had been sent to announce the departure. Indian officials also seized the Portuguese merchandise. Men and merchandise were hostages for the money.

Vasco da Gama was never more dangerous than when he was threatened. He bided his time and made no reply to the Zamorin's demand. Even after Monçaide, the "good" Moor, told him of a plot to destroy the fleet, Vasco continued to entertain Indians on his ships, to feed the poor, and to wait—until some men who seemed to be of high rank visited him.

Then, as the *Log-Book* narrates below, Vasco da Gama acted ruthlessly to insure the safety of the fleet.

On . . . Sunday [August 19] about twenty-five men came [to the ships]. Among them were six persons of quality, and the captain perceived that through these we might recover the men who were detained as prisoners on land. He therefore laid hands upon them, and upon a dozen of the others, being eighteen in all.

The rest he ordered to be landed in one of his boats, and gave them a letter to be delivered to the king's Moorish factor, in which he declared that if he would restore the men who were being kept prisoners he would liberate those whom he had taken. . . .

On Thursday, the 23rd, of the same month, we made sail, saying we were going to Portugal, but hoped to be back soon. . . . We anchored about four leagues to the leeward of Calicut, and we did this because of the headwind. . . .

When the king heard that we had sailed for Portugal, and that he was thus no longer able to carry his point, he thought of undoing the evil he had done. He sent for Diogo Dias, whom he received with marked kindness. . . . He asked why the captain had carried off these men.

Diogo Dias said it was because the king would not allow him and his to return to the ships, and detained them as prisoners in the city.

The king said he had done well. He then asked whether his factor had asked for anything, giving us to understand that he was ignorant of the matter, and that the factor alone was responsible for this extortion [the request for customs charges]. . . .

The king then said: "Go you back to the ships, you and the others who are with you; tell the captain to send me back the men he took; that the pillar, which I understood him to say he desires to be erected on the land shall be taken away by those who bring you back, and put up; and, moreover, that you will remain here with the merchandise."

At the same time he [the king] forwarded a letter

to the captain, which had been written for him by Diogo Dias with an iron pen upon a palm leaf, as is the custom of the country, and which was intended for the King of Portugal. The tenor of this letter was as follows:

"Vasco da Gama, a gentleman of your household, came to my country, whereat I was pleased. My country is rich in cinnamon, cloves, ginger, pepper, and precious stones. That which I ask of you in exchange is gold, silver, corals and scarlet cloth."

On Monday, the 27th of this month, in the morning, whilst we were at anchor, seven boats with many people in them brought Diogo Dias and the other Portuguese who were with him. Not daring to put him on board, they placed him in the captain's longboat, which was still attached to the stern. They had not brought the merchandise, for they believed that Diogo Dias would return with them. But once the captain had them [Dias and the other Portuguese] back on board, he would not allow them to return to the land.

The pillar he gave to those in the boat, as the king had given orders for it to be set up. He [Vasco da Gama] also gave up, in exchange, the six most distinguished among his prisoners, keeping six others, whom he promised to surrender if on the morrow the merchandise were restored to him. . . .

On Wednesday, the 29th [of August], the captain-major and the other captains agreed that, inasmuch that we had discovered the country we had come in search of, as also spices and precious stones, and it appeared impossible to establish cordial relations with the people, it would be a well to take our departure. And it was resolved that we should take with us the men whom we detained, as, on our return to Calicut, they might be useful to us in establishing friendly relations.

We therefore set sail and left for Portugal, greatly rejoicing at our good fortune in having made so great a discovery.

On Thursday [August 30], at noon, being becalmed about a league . . . [north of] Calicut, about seventy boats approached us. They were crowded with people wearing a kind of cuirass [breastplate] made of red cloth, folded. . . . When these boats came within the range of our bombards, the captain-major ordered us to fire upon them.

They followed us for about an hour and a half, when there arose a thunderstorm which carried us out to sea; and when they saw they could no longer do us harm they turned back, whilst we pursued our route.

A Fearful Voyage

As the Portuguese set out once more across the great plain of the sea, Vasco da Gama led them on a northwest course along the coast of India. They stopped once, to land one of the six hostages Vasco da Gama was carrying back to Portugal; Vasco gave this man a letter to the Zamorin "explaining" the kidnaping of the other five.

Opposite the city of Goa, in the Angediva Islands, they careened and repaired their ships, and skirmished with pirates. Then the prows of the *St. Gabriel*, the *St. Raphael*, and the *Berrio* were pointed toward Africa.

Because the Portuguese had not waited until November for the favoring northeast monsoon, they had a fearful voyage across the Indian Ocean. Opposing winds and calms made the trip interminable—ninety days, compared to the twenty-seven-day run on the outward journey. The sailors became weak, sallow, and short of breath. All their muscles ached, and their gums began to bleed. Scurvy, the dread disease caused by their poor diet of partially spoiled meat and biscuit, afflicted them.

(Not until 1795, when the British Navy made lime juice a regular part of its rations at sea, did mariners learn how to avoid scurvy on long voyages. British sailors were nicknamed "Limeys" because of their lime juice.)

The *Log-Book* below describes the crossing from India. Mogadishu, where the surviving Portuguese struck the African coast just above the equator, was a fortified town with fine houses, probably the first settlement made by Arab traders when they began their push south in the thirteenth century.

Owing to frequent calms and foul winds it took us three months less three days to cross this gulf [the Indian Ocean], and all our people again suffered from their gums, which grew over their teeth, so that they could not eat. Their legs also swelled, and other parts of the body, and these swellings spread until the sufferer died, without exhibiting symptoms of any other disease.

Thirty of our men died in this manner—an equal number having died previously—and those able to navigate each ship were only seven or eight, and even these were not as well as they ought to have been. I assure you that if this state of affairs had continued for another fortnight, there would have been no men at all to navigate the ships. We had come to such a pass that all bonds of discipline had gone.

Whilst suffering this affliction we addressed vows and petitions to the saints on behalf of our ships. The captains had held council, and they had agreed that if a favorable wind enabled us we would return to India whence we had come.

But it pleased God in his mercy to send us a wind which, in the course of six days, carried us within sight of land, and at this we rejoiced as much as if the land we saw had been Portugal, for with the help of God we hoped to recover our health there. . . .

This happened on January 2, 1499. It was night when we came close to the land, and for this reason we put about ship and lay to. In the morning [January 3] we reconnoitered the coast, so as to find out whither the Lord had taken us. . . .

We found ourselves off a large town, with houses of several stories, big palaces in its center, and four towers around it. This town faced the sea, belonged to the Moors, and was called Mogadishu. When we were quite close to it we fired off many bombards, and continued along the coast with a fair wind. We went on thus during the day, but lay to at night, as we did not know how far we were from Malindi whither we wished to go.

On Saturday, the 5th of the month, being becalmed, a thunderstorm burst upon us, and tore the ties of the *Raphael.* Whilst repairing these a privateer came out from a town called Pate with eight boats and many men, but as soon as he came within reach of our bombards we fired upon him, and he fled. There being no wind we were not able to follow him.

On Monday, the 7th [of January], we again cast anchor off Malindi, when the king at once sent off to us a longboat holding many people, with a present of sheep, and a message to the captain-major, bidding him welcome. . . .

The captain-major . . . sent a present to the king, and also a message . . . begging for a tusk of ivory to be given to the King of Portugal, his Lord, and asking that a pillar [*padrão*] be placed on the land as a sign of friendship. The king replied that he would do what was asked out of love for the King of Portugal. . . .

We remained five days at this place enjoying ourselves, and reposing from the hardships endured during a passage in the course of which all of us had been face to face with death.

Homeward Bound

The journey back always seems shorter than the trip out. So it was for Vasco da Gama and his brave seamen after they left Malindi.

They stopped at some sand banks just south of Mombasa, on which the *St. Raphael* had been grounded on the voyage to India, and there burned this same ship because they lacked the men to sail it. Among the goods which they transferred from it to the other ships was the brightly painted figurehead of the ship itself. Today this carved image of St. Raphael is preserved in the Abbey of the Jeronimos, outside Lisbon, where Vasco da Gama is buried.

At an island near Mozambique, Vasco da Gama set up his fourth and last stone pillar. Then, in a fair wind, the fleet doubled the Cape of Good Hope. Two ships in place of four, fewer than one hundred men, in place of the original 170, were homeward bound.

We left [Malindi] on Friday [January 11, 1499], in the morning, and on Saturday, which was the 12th of the month, we passed close to Mombasa. On Sunday [January 13] we anchored at the *Baixos de S. Raphael*, [Shoals of St. Raphael], where we set fire to the ship of that name, as it was impossible for us to navigate three vessels with the few hands that remained to us. The contents of this ship were transferred to the two other ships. . . .

On Sunday, the 27th, we left this place with a fair wind. During the following night we lay to, and in the morning [January 28] we came close to a large island called Zanzibar, which is peopled by Moors,

and is quite ten leagues from the mainland. Late on February 1, we anchored off the island of S. Jorge, near Mozambique.

On the following day [February 2], in the morning, we set up a pillar in that island, where we had said mass on going out. The rain fell so heavily that we could not light a fire for melting the lead to fix the cross [to the top of the pillar], and it therefore remained without one. We then returned to the ships.

On March 3 we reached the Angra de São Bras [Mossel Bay], where we caught many anchovies, seals and penguins, which we salted for our voyage. On the 12th we left, but when ten or twelve leagues from the watering place the wind blew so strongly from the west that we were compelled to return to this bay.

When the wind fell we started once more, and the Lord gave us such a good wind that on the 20th we were able to double the Cape of Good Hope. Those who had come so far were in good health and quite robust, although at times nearly dead from the cold winds which we experienced. This feeling, however, we attributed less to the cold than to the heat of the countries from which we had come.

We pursued our route with a great desire of reaching home. For twenty-seven days we had the wind astern, and were carried by it to the neighborhood of the island of Santiago [in the Cape Verde Islands]. . . .

But the wind fell and we were becalmed. The little wind there was came from ahead. Thunderstorms, which came from the land, enabled us to tell our whereabouts, and we plied to windward as well as we could. . . .

A few words more, and the *Log-Book* breaks off. One theory is that the seaman-author disembarked at a Portuguese settlement at Sierra Leone, the rugged mountains capped by rumbling thunderheads along the Guinea Coast.

The *St. Gabriel* and the *Berrio* became separated in a storm. Each plowed its lonely way through the Atlantic, carrying the spices of the East to Europe by a new route.

Exciting News

After the two remaining ships became separated, the *St. Gabriel* landed at Santiago, in the Cape Verde Islands. Paul da Gama, wan and spitting blood, was dying of tuberculosis. Vasco turned the *St. Gabriel* over to his clerk, John da Sá, with orders to proceed to Portugal, while he anxiously chartered a swift caravel for himself and Paul.

The caravel left immediately for Lisbon, heading out into the Atlantic to avoid opposing currents off the African coast. Near the Azores, however, Paul was barely conscious. Vasco became terrified at the thought of burying his brother at sea and had to land. Here at Terceira Island, in the Azores, kindly Paul died and was buried in the monastery of St. Francis. Vasco da Gama was numb with grief.

Meanwhile the *Berrio*, under Nicholas Coelho, had reached Lisbon on July 10, 1499. Vasco da Gama, mourning for Paul, sailed on and crossed the bar of Lisbon Harbor August 29, 1499.

Immediately after Coelho arrived, King Manuel wrote

the following triumphant letter to his neighbor monarchs, Ferdinand and Isabella. Now Portugal had someone to match or surpass Spain's Columbus!

Most high and excellent Prince and Princess, most potent Lord and Lady!

Your Highnesses already know that we had ordered Vasco da Gama, a nobleman of our household, and his brother Paul da Gama, with four vessels to make discoveries by sea, and that two years have now elapsed since their departure. And as the principal motive of this enterprise has been, with our predecessors, the service of God our Lord, and our own advantage, it pleased Him in His mercy to speed them on their route.

From a message which has now been brought to this city by one of the captains, we learn that they did reach and discover India and other kingdoms and lordships bordering upon it; that they entered and navigated its sea, finding large cities, large edifices and rivers, and great populations, among whom is carried on all the trade in spices and precious stones, which are forwarded in ships . . . to Mecca, and thence to Cairo, whence they are dispersed throughout the world.

Of these spices, etc., they have brought a quantity, including cinnamon, cloves, ginger, nutmeg, and pepper, as well as other kinds, together with the boughs and leaves of the same; also many fine stones of all sorts, such as rubies and others. And they also came to a country in which there are mines of gold, of which gold, as of the spices and precious stones, they did not bring as much as they could have done, for they took no merchandise with them.

As we are aware that your Highnesses will hear of these things with much pleasure and satisfaction, we thought well to give this information. And your Highnesses may believe . . . concerning the Christian people whom these explorers reached, that it will be possible, notwithstanding that they are not as yet strong in the faith or possessed of a thorough knowledge of it, to do much in the service of God and the exaltation of the Holy Faith, once they shall have been converted and fully fortified (confirmed) in it.

And when they shall have thus been fortified in the faith there will be an opportunity for destroying the Moors of those parts. Moreover, we hope, with the help of God, that the great trade which now enriches the Moors of those parts . . . shall . . . be diverted to the natives and ships of our own kingdom, so that henceforth all Christendom, in this part of Europe, shall be able, in a large measure, to provide itself with these spices and precious stones. . . .

Most high and excellent Prince and Princess, most potent Lord and Lady, may the Lord our God ever hold your persons and kingdoms in His holy keeping.

Written at Lisbon, July, 1499.

King Manuel's exultation was well founded. The immediate results of Vasco da Gama's voyage were far greater than those of Columbus's Atlantic crossing. Columbus had discovered little more than naked savages and grass huts, but Vasco da Gama had found his way to the riches of the Orient.

A Hero's Welcome

On September 8, 1499, King Manuel sent a great procession to escort Vasco da Gama from Belem, outside Lisbon, to his palace. Cannon roared, banners flaunted, and Count de Meneses, in silk and gold, accompanied by many nobles, led the tired da Gama, whose black beard had not been cut since he departed, through a multitude of people into the court.

Holding his letter from the Zamorin, Vasco da Gama knelt before the king.

"Sire, all my hardships have come to an end at this moment," he said, "since the Lord has brought me to the presence of your Highness."

Manuel put his arm around Vasco's shoulders and raised him.

"For my sake, console yourself for the death of your brother," said King Manuel. "His affairs shall not suffer."

Manuel promised that the same recompense owing to Paul would be made to his relatives. The king was overjoyed; he could imagine the dismay which da Gama's achievement would bring to the merchants of Venice and the Sultan of Egypt. His large, staring eyes shone, as though at this moment he could see the downcast faces of the Doge, Council, and merchants of Venice, could hear the heartfelt curses of the Sultan of Egypt.

For the balance of power was now beginning to shift from Italy and the Mediterranean to the Atlantic. The Moslems were about to suffer a mortal blow: the threat of the Ottoman Turks to Europe would diminish as their trade with the East declined. The epic quest of Prince

Henry, Diogo Cão, John II, and Bartholomew Dias had finally succeeded, by means of the most difficult feat of navigation yet recorded.

Vasco da Gama had sailed six thousand miles to India, over the very best sea road, and had returned with the samples of ivory, gold, gems, and spices which would fire Portuguese hearts for the winning of an empire.

"Lord of the Conquest, Navigation and Commerce of Ethiopia, Arabia, Persia, and India" was the new title adopted by King Manuel.

"Admiral of the Indian Seas" was the rank awarded Vasco da Gama.

6

Caravels Win an Empire

The Portuguese entered India with the sword in one hand and the Crucifix in the other; finding much gold they laid aside the Crucifix to fill their pockets.

—John de Castro, Portuguese Viceroy of India

The "Gold Rush" to the Indies

When Gil Eannes came back from doubling Cape Bojador, he brought Prince Henry the Navigator an armful of roses, picked on the rocky shore below the cape. Later captains returned with more substantial, less poetic, winnings: slaves, gold, and now spices. After Vasco da Gama's voyage the Portuguese, hoping to make their fortunes, rushed to enlist for the next expedition to the East.

King Manuel planned to exploit the new route to India immediately. He prepared a fleet of thirteen ships, all larger than any of Vasco da Gama's four and laden with better merchandise than da Gama had carried. The purpose was frankly commercial: to secure trade treaties at Calicut and other Indian cities, and to bring back a profitable cargo of spices.

Vasco da Gama, recently married and still saddened by the loss of his brother Paul, declined the command of the expedition. King Manuel then turned to a poised, idealistic young nobleman, Pedro Alvares Cabral, who believed, like King Manuel, that God Himself had guided the Portuguese to India. (There is no evidence that Cabral had ever been on a voyage before.)

Cabral's fleet had supplies for twelve hundred men for a year and a half. Although preoccupied with profits, King Manuel did not overlook religion: several Franciscan friars went to better instruct the "Christians" of Calicut, and the devout Cabral carried an image of the Blessed Virgin Mary. Among the captains and pilots were such outstanding navigators as Bartholomew Dias, Nicolas Coelho, Diogo Dias, Pero Escolar, and Duarte Pacheco Pereira.

An independent official, Ayres Correia, with two assistant factors, was in charge of the cargo, which included copper, coral, mercury, woolen cloth, satins, and velvets.

On March 9, 1500, the fleet sailed from Lisbon. Cabral

carried instructions from King Manuel and a letter from the king to the Zamorin of Calicut. He also had a "road map," a brief list of directions dictated by Vasco da Gama, recommending the southwest course to the Cape of Good Hope, the course da Gama had followed. These directions are printed below.

This is the way which it appears to Vasco da Gama that Pedro Alvares [Cabral] should follow on his voyage, if it please Our Lord.

In the first place, before he departs from here [Lisbon], to make very good ordinance so that the ships will not be lost some from the others, in this manner: namely, whenever they are obliged to change their course, the chief captain shall make two fires, and all shall respond to him, each with two similar fires. And after they thus respond to him they shall all turn. . . .

Some instructions about raising and lowering sails are omitted here.

After in good time they depart from here [Lisbon], they will make their course straight to the island of Santiago [in the Cape Verde Islands], and if at the time that they arrive there, they have sufficient water for four months, they need not stop . . . but when they have the wind behind them make their way toward the south. And if they must vary their course let it be in the southwest direction. And as soon as they meet with a light wind they should take a circular course until they put the Cape of Good Hope directly east.

And from then on they are to navigate as the weather serves them, and they gain more, because when they are in the said parallel, with the aid of Our Lord, they will not lack weather with which they may round the aforesaid Cape. And in this manner it appears to him that the navigation will be shortest and the ships more secure from worms, and in this way even the food will be kept better and the people will be healthier.

The "worms" mentioned above were wood-boring teredos, a kind of sea-going termite which might eat the bottom of a ship so full of holes that it would sink. Teredos sank one of Columbus's ships on his fourth voyage to America.

And if it happens, and may it please God that it will not, that any of these ships become separated from the captain, then it must sail as well as it can to make the Cape and go to the watering place of São Bras [Mossel Bay]. And if it gets here before the captain it should anchor in a good position and wait for him, because it is necessary for the chief captain to go there to take on water so that henceforth he may have nothing to do with the land, but keep away from it until Mozambique for the health of his men. . . .

And if it be the case that the chief captain comes

first to this watering place, before the ship or ships
which are lost from him . . .

The original manuscript breaks off here.

The Land of Vera Cruz

A traveler crossing Death Valley would be astounded to
come upon a metropolis resembling New York. Cabral
and his men were just as astonished when, after only six
weeks at sea, they sighted a round, lofty mountain, then
green forests and a flat coast broken by the mouth of a
river. Following da Gama's course, they had thought they
were in the midst of the Ocean Sea—but instead they had
bumped into Brazil!

Cabral named the new country Terra da Vera Cruz
("Land of the True Cross") because for many nights he
had been seeing the bright Southern Cross in the sky. The
flag of Brazil today shows the stars of the Southern Cross
in honor of this name. Since Cabral arrived just after
Easter, he called the lofty mountain Monte Pascoal
("Easter Mountain"); he named the harbor in which they
later anchored, behind a reef, Porto Seguro ("Safe Port").
They were about six hundred miles north of Rio de
Janeiro.

Churchmen preferred to call the country Terra de
Santa Cruz ("Land of the Holy Cross"), while common
seamen, startled by the squawks of macaws, dubbed the
land Terra de Papagaios ("Parrot Land"). However, by
mid-century "Brazil," the name of a red dye-wood which
was for years the country's best known product, had
been adopted. ("Brazil" was also the name of a legendary
Atlantic island.)

Although he was not certain whether he had found an
island or a continent, Cabral had letters describing his dis-

covery sent to Lisbon on the supply ship. The selection below is taken from the most detailed of these letters, written by the cavalier Vaz de Caminha to King Manuel.

Senhor:

Although the chief captain of this your fleet, and also the other captains, are writing to Your Highness the news of the finding of this your new land which was now found in this navigation, I shall not refrain from also giving my account of this to Your Highness, as best I can. . . .

We followed our route over this sea [the Atlantic] until Tuesday . . . the 21st of April, [1500], when we came upon some signs of land, being then distant from the [Cape Verde Islands], as the pilots said, some six hundred and sixty or six hundred and seventy leagues; these signs were a great quantity of long weeds which mariners call *botelho* [bottle], and others as well which they also call *rabo de asno* [donkey's tail]. And on the following Wednesday, in the morning, we met with birds which they call *fura buchos* [petrels].

On this day at the vesper hours we caught sight of land, that is, first of a large mountain, very high and round, and of other lower lands to the south of it, and of flat land, with great groves of trees. To this high mountain the captain gave the name of Monte Pascoal [Easter Mountain], and to the land, Terra da Vera Cruz [Land of the True Cross]. . . .

At sunset, some six leagues from the land, we cast anchor. . . .

This land . . . is so great that it will have some twenty or twenty-five leagues of coastline. Along the shore in some places it has great banks, some of them red, some white, and the land above is quite flat and covered with great forests. From point to point the entire shore is very flat and very beautiful.

As for the interior, it appeared to us from the sea very large, for, as far as eye could reach, we could see only land and forests, a land which seemed very extensive to us. Up to now we are unable to learn that there is gold or silver in it, or anything of metal or iron; nor have we seen any, but the land itself has a very good climate, as cold and temperate as that of Entre-Douro-e-Minho [a province in north Portugal], because in the present season we found it like that. Its waters are quite endless . . . everything will grow in it because of its waters. . . .

If there were nothing more than to have here a stopping place for this voyage to Calicut, that would suffice.

Pedro Vaz de Caminha

Cabral's landing in Brazil has suggested to historians that the Portuguese would have discovered America even if Columbus had never lived. The best sea route to India swung so close to Brazil, out around the Guinea doldrums and the opposing southeast trade winds, that sooner or later a Portuguese ship bound for Calicut would have sighted South America.

Columbus himself would not have succeeded without the knowledge he acquired from the Portuguese, in the Azores and on a voyage he made with them to Guinea. "It was in Portugal that the Admiral [Columbus] began to think that if men could sail so far south, one might also sail west and find lands in that quarter," said his son Ferdinand.

Indians, Hammocks, Parrots

The Indians who greeted Cabral and his men were called Tupi or Guarani; they were a branch of the fierce and handsome Caribs, who gave their name to the Caribbean Sea. (The Caribals, or Canibals, were so fond of eating their slain enemies that we derive our word *cannibal* from them, also.) The Tupi-Guarani, still in the Stone Age culture, gained their living by hunting and fishing. They were skilled swimmers who could attack and kill a shark by thrusting a pointed stick down its throat.

The Indians were friendly. Vaz de Caminha told how Diogo Dias, "an agreeable and pleasure-loving man . . . took with him one of our bagpipe players and his bagpipe, and began to dance among them, taking them by the hands, and they were delighted and laughed and accompanied him very well to the sound of the pipe." Caminha also described how the Indians "traded there, for bells and for other trifles of little value . . . very large and beautiful red parrots and two little green ones and caps of green feathers and a cloth of feathers of many colors, woven in a very beautiful fashion."

These Indians are further described below, in a passage taken from the *Anonymous Narrative*, an account of Cabral's voyage by an unknown but observant member of the fleet. The *Anonymous Narrative* was first printed in 1507, in the *Paesi Novamente Retrovati* (*New Found Lands*), the book by which the news of the exploits of Columbus, da Gama, and others was spread throughout Europe.

In appearance these people are dark, and they go nude without shame, and their hair is long, and they pluck their beards. And their eyelids and over their eyebrows are painted with figures of white and black and blue and red. They have the lip of the mouth, that is, the lower lip, pierced. In the opening they put a bone as large as a nail, and others wear there a long blue stone or a green one, and they hang from their lips. Women likewise go nude without shame and they are beautiful of body, with long hair.

And their houses are of wood, covered with leaves and branches of trees, with many wooden columns. In the middle of the said houses and from the said columns to the wall they hang a net [hammock] of cotton, which holds a man. And between the nets they make a fire. Thus in a single house there may be forty or fifty beds set up like looms.

In this land we saw no iron nor any other metal. They cut wood with stone. And they have many birds of many sorts, especially parrots, of many colors; among them are some as large as hens; and there are other very beautiful birds. Of the feathers of the said birds they make the hats and caps which they wear.

A Great Storm

After an eleven-day stopover, Cabral's fleet departed, May 2, 1500, from Brazil. Two Portuguese convicts were left behind, weeping, to collect more information about the land, and the ships sailed south and southeast, toward the Cape of Good Hope. As they came into latitude 30° to 32° south, they entered the high pressure area of the South Atlantic, a breeding place of hurricanes.

The *Anonymous Narrative*, below, tells what followed.

The following day, which was the 2nd of May of the said year [1500], the armada made sail on its way to go round the Cape of Good Hope. This voyage would be across the gulf of the sea more than 1,200 leagues. . . . On the 12th day of the said month, while on our course, there appeared a comet with a very long tail in the direction of Arabia. It was in view continuously for eight or ten nights.

On Sunday, which was the 24th day . . . of May, as all the armada was sailing together with a favorable wind, with the sails half set and without bonnets because of a rain which we had the day before, while we were thus sailing, there came on us a head wind so strong and so sudden that we knew nothing of it until the sails were across the masts. And at that moment four ships were lost with all on board, without our being able to give them aid in any way.

Among the most tragic of the losses was that of faithful

Bartholomew Dias, who perished almost within sight of the majestic headland which he had discovered twelve years before. As his ship foundered, the Cape loomed in the distance—not King John's "Cape of Good Hope," but the grim mass which, prophetically, Dias had called "The Cape of Storms."

The other seven ships which escaped were also almost lost. And thus we took the wind astern with the masts and sails broken. And we were at the mercy of God; and thus we went all that day. The sea was so swollen that it seemed that we were mounting up to the heavens.

The wind changed suddenly, although the storm was still so great that we had no desire to set sails to the wind. And going thus with this storm, without sails, we lost sight of one another, so that the ship of the captain with two others took a different route. And another ship called *Il Re* with two others took another route, and the other one, alone, took still another. And thus we went twenty days through this storm without setting a sail to the wind.

Six of Cabral's seven surviving ships came together again at Mozambique, on the East African coast, and proceeded to Calicut. The seventh, which took a route "alone," was blown so far east that its crew sighted the great island of Madagascar, not previously visited by Europeans. Captain

Diogo Dias named it "The Isle of St. Lawrence" because it was first seen on August 10, the saint's feast day.

Diogo Dias never did reach India. He sailed as far as the Red Sea, becoming the first European to travel to Somaliland by sea; then he turned back and rejoined the fleet on its homeward voyage.

The Bombardment of Calicut

For several hundred years the Arabs had monopolized the world's richest trade. They had sent their small, unarmed dhows swarming across the Indian Ocean, carrying porcelain and silks from China, spices, myrrh, and frankincense from the Malay Peninsula and Indonesia, and ivory, gold, peacocks, and ambergris from East Africa. When the second Portuguese expedition in two years arrived before Calicut and demanded special trading privileges, the Arab merchants determined to fight to protect their monopoly.

With his cannon trained on Calicut through the black portholes of his ships, Cabral anchored in the roadstead, forced the Zamorin to send him hostages, and finally secured from the evasive ruler permission to establish a Portuguese factory (trading post) on shore. During these negotiations the Portuguese at last realized that the Hindu Indians were not Christians.

Then, as the *Anonymous Narrative* relates below, the Arabs and fanatical Moplahs struck, with or without the Zamorin's consent. They instigated a riot which led to a fiery reprisal by Cabral and the beginning of war in the East.

After we had been in the land [Calicut] about three months and the treaty had been signed and two of our ships loaded with spices, the captain [Cabral] one day sent on shore to tell the king [the Zamorin] that he [Cabral] had been in his land for three months and had loaded only two ships, and that the Moors were concealing the merchandise from them and the ships of Mecca were secretly loading and were thus departing, and that the said captain would be greatly obliged to him [the Zamorin] if he would have this attended to with dispatch, because the time of his [Cabral's] departure was already approaching.

The king replied to him that he would be given all the merchandise he wished, and that no Moorish ship would be allowed to load until our ships were loaded, and if any Moorish ship should leave that the captain might take it to see whether the ship had any merchandise, and that he would have it given to them at the price which the said Moors had paid for it.

On the 16th day of December of the said year [1500], as Ayres Correia was settling accounts with two factors and writers of two of our ships which were already loaded for departure, a Moorish ship left with much merchandise. The captain took it, and the captain of that Moorish ship, and the most honorable of his men among them disembarked and made great lamentation and uproar, so that all the Moors assembled and went to talk with the king, telling how we had on land more riches than we had carried to his kingdom, and that we were the worst robbers and thieves in the world, that as we had taken their ship in his port so would we do from that day onward, and that they were obliged to kill all and that His Highness should rob the house of the factor [the Portuguese factory, or trading post].

The king . . . agreed that this should be done. And we, not knowing anything of this, allowed some of our men to go on shore to do their trading throughout the city.

Although the Portuguese blamed the Hindu Zamorin, historians are not certain whether or not he actually conspired with the Arabs in the attack on the trading post.

We saw all the people [the Arabs] come against our men, slaughtering them and wounding them; and the rest of us went to give them aid; so that on that shore we slew seven or eight of them, and they two or three of us. And we were about seventy men with swords and helmets, and they were innumerable, with lances and swords and shields and bows and arrows. And they so pressed us that it was necessary to retreat to the house [the "factory" or trading post]; and during the retreat they wounded five or six men.

And thus we closed the door with much effort, and they fought against the house even though it was surrounded by a wall as high as a man on horseback. We had seven or eight crossbows with which we killed a mountain of people. More than three thousand of their warriors assembled.

And we raised a banner so that those on the ships might send us aid. The boats drew near the shore, and from there they fired their bombards and did no damage.

Then the Moors began to break down the wall of the house so that in the space of an hour they razed it entirely. They sounded trumpets and drums with great shouts and pleasure, so that it seemed as though the king were with them because we saw one of his attendants. And Ayres Correia saw that we had no remedy whatever, and because we had been fighting for two hours so fiercely that our men could hold out no longer, he determined that we should sally forth to the shore, breaking through them to see whether the boats might not save us.

We did this. And thus the greater part of our men arrived near enough to enter the water, and the boats did not dare to approach to receive us. And thus, because of little assistance, Ayres Correia was slain and with him fifty and more men. And we escaped by swimming, to the number of twenty persons, all severely wounded. Among these a son of the aforesaid Ayres Correia escaped; he must have been about eleven years old.

Thus we entered the boats, almost drowned. The captain of the said boats was Sancho de Tovar, because the chief captain [Cabral] was sick. And thus they took us to the ship.

And when the chief captain saw this dissension and bad treatment, he ordered ten Moorish ships which were in the port to be taken, and all the people whom we found in the said ships to be killed. And thus we slew to the number of five hundred or six hundred men, and captured twenty or thirty who were hiding in the holds of the ships and also merchandise; and thus we robbed the ships and took what they had within them. One had in it three elephants which we killed and ate; and we burned all nine of the unloaded ships.

And the following day our ships drew nearer to land and bombarded the city [Calicut], so that we slew an endless number of people and did them much damage, and they fired from on shore with very weak bombards. . . .

[Then] the captain [Cabral] quickly decided that we should go to Cochin, where we might load the ships.

Cabral's bombardment of relatively defenseless Calicut left the harbor and city strewn with wreckage, the people terrorized, and the Zamorin consumed with hatred for the Portuguese. But other cities on the Malabar Coast which had been oppressed by the Zamorin rejoiced. Cochin, one hundred miles to the south, welcomed Cabral and provided spices for his ships, as did Cananore, just north of Calicut.

Cabral thus began the Portuguese policy of making alliances with subject rulers against Calicut. His fleet reached

Lisbon in June and July, 1501, with a cargo of spices which returned 100 per cent profits to investors.

Vasco da Gama Returns to India

In 1502 King Manuel sent Vasco da Gama, whose spirit had darkened since Paul's death, with a fleet of twenty ships to take revenge on the Zamorin. Da Gama carried out the king's orders with great cruelty.

Near Cananore, for example, he took a rich Arabian ship, the *Meri*, crowded with 380 pilgrims returning from Mecca, the holy city of Mohammedans. Da Gama sent his seamen leaping aboard the captured vessel to snatch jewels, gold, and other wealth from the passengers and herd them all into the hold. Then he had the ship set on fire.

Women held up babies in their arms, pleading for mercy, but da Gama stood unmoved, a short, somber figure with hands on hips, watching through a porthole in his cabin. When screaming Arabs clawed their way up through the hatches, the Portuguese drove them back. All but twenty were burned to death.

Da Gama then proceeded to Calicut, where he demanded peremptorily that the Zamorin expel every Moslem from the city. The Zamorin refused.

"I could carve a better king than you out of a palm tree," Vasco told the Zamorin.

Then he bombarded the city for two days, and took the further horrible revenge described below. Probably his sailors never forgot the Hindu death chants, wailed in the light of smoky torches over the poor, dismembered fishermen.

Vasco da Gama's exploits on his second voyage to India were recorded by an anonymous Flemish seaman who served under him. The following selection is from this brief Flemish narrative, *Calcoen* [Calicut], first published in 1504 in Antwerp.

[At Cape St. Mary] we put our things in order, and we had still to cross a gulf [the Arabian Sea] which is well 700 miles wide. There . . . we shaped our course to the northeast.

It must be known that there . . . all the time from April to September . . . the wind blows from the southeast. . . . And from September to April . . . the wind blows during the whole time from the northeast. . . . And as is the wind so is the current. . . .

On the 5th day of August [1502] we saw the Polar Star, and were very glad of it, for we were still more than 500 miles from India.

In fifteen days we sailed across the great gulf of 770 miles, and it was on the 21st day of August [1502] we saw the land of India, and saw a great city called Cambay. . . .

Near the land beyond High Arabia is the town of Mecca, where is buried Mahomet, the devil of the pagans. . . . We passed beyond a town called Goa . . . and we took 400 ships from Goa, and we killed the people and burnt the ships.

Thence we sailed and arrived in an island called Angediva; there we took in water and wood, and we landed at least 300 of our invalids, and we killed a lizard [crocodile] which was at least five feet long.

On the 11th day of September [1502] we arrived in a kingdom called Cananore, and it is situate near a chain of mountains called Mont Ely, and there we watched the ships of Mecca, and they are ships which carry the spices which come to our country, and we spoiled the woods, so that the King of Portugal alone should get spices from there. . . .

At the same time we took a Mecca ship, on board of which were 380 men and many women and children, and we took from it at least 12,000 ducats and at least 10,000 more worth of goods, and we burnt the ship and all the people on board with gunpowder, on the first day of October. . . .

On the 27th day of October [1502] we sailed thence, and arrived in a kingdom called Calicut, which is 40 miles from Cananore, and we mustered our forces before the town, and we fought with them during three days, and we took a great number of people, and we hanged them to the yards of the ships, and taking them down, we cut off their hands, feet, and heads; and we took one of their ships and threw into it the hands, feet, and heads, and we wrote a letter, which we put on a stick, and we left that ship to go adrift toward the land. . . .

On the 2nd day of November [1502] we sailed from Calicut 60 miles to a kingdom called Cochin . . . [where] we went . . . to speak with the king. And the king came to us in great state, bringing with him six war elephants; for he has many elephants in his country, and many strange animals which I do not know. Then our chiefs which we had with us spoke to the king, in order to buy spices and other things.

After loading spices at Cochin, Vasco da Gama returned to Calicut for a battle with the Zamorin's small vessels, which quickly fled, and then he sailed back to Portugal.

Almeida's Armada

Vasco da Gama's second voyage to India resulted in a new trade treaty for Portugal (with Cochin) and more profits, but did not end the struggle for supremacy in the East. In 1503, in Cochin, the Portuguese built their first fortress, which Duarte Pacheco Pereira and ninety soldiers successfully defended against sixty thousand of the Zamorin's men. Every year King Manuel sent a new expedition to India.

But leaving factories guarded only by a handful of soldiers between expeditions was like having a candy booth untended at a fair. In 1505, therefore, King Manuel created the office of Viceroy of India and sent forty-five-year-old Francisco de Almeida, a gallant and experienced naval commander, to the East on a three-year appointment.

Almeida was to erect fortresses in East Africa and western India to control hostile territory, much as we established cavalry posts in the prairies a hundred years ago. His ships would remain in the East instead of returning, as Portuguese fleets always had returned, with the winter monsoon.

"Avoid the annexation of territory," Almeida, a champion of sea power, advised the king. "Build no more fortresses than may be absolutely necessary to protect your factories from a sudden raid; we can spare no men from the navy."

Almeida was right; the issue was to be decided at sea,

and soon. Even as he sailed, in March, 1505, the conflict was heading for a showdown. Less than half as many spices were now shipped by way of Alexandria and Venice as had been before 1502, and the Sultan of Egypt, whose profits as middleman were 33 per cent of every cargo, was losing hundreds of thousands of dollars. Furious at his losses, the sultan, aided by Venice, determined to build a great fleet on the Red Sea and sweep the Portuguese from the Indian Ocean.

When Almeida's twenty-two ships, bearing fifteen hundred soldiers and four hundred artillerymen, reached Cochin, in November, 1505, the Zamorin of Calicut acted without awaiting the arrival of the Egyptian fleet. Almeida's son Don Lourenço, whom the Viceroy had sent north with a task force of eleven ships, discovered the Zamorin's plans by accident.

Don Lourenço, an eighteen-year-old giant and the most feared swordsman in Portugal, was sitting one day in the fortress at Cananore when a stranger dressed in an Arab burnoose approached and offered him information about the Zamorin.

The stranger identified himself as Ludovico Varthema, an Italian who had wandered across Arabia and India. He reported that the Zamorin had collected a large fleet with which to attack the Portuguese.

Don Lourenço immediately set sail. A few weeks later he intercepted the Indian fleet of 209 vessels off Cananore. Varthema, who had joined the Portuguese, describes below the sea fight which followed (March 16–17, 1506). This selection is taken from Varthema's *Travels*, first published in 1510 in Rome.

[On March 12, 1506] the immense [Arab-Indian] fleet departed from . . . Calicut [and several ports near Calicut]. All this fleet was 209 sail, of which eighty-four were large ships, and the remainder were rowing vessels, that is, *paraos*.

In which fleet there was an infinite number of armed Moors; and they wore certain red garments of cloth stuffed with cotton, and they wore certain large caps stuffed, and also on the arms bracelets and gloves stuffed; and a great number of bows and lances, swords and shields, and large and small artillery after our custom.

When we saw this fleet, which was on the 16th of the month above-mentioned, truly, seeing so many ships together, it appeared as though one saw a very large wood. We Christians always hoped that God would aid us to confound the Pagan faith. And the most valiant knight, the captain of the fleet [Don Lourenço], son of Don Francisco de Almeida, Viceroy of India, was here with eleven ships, amongst which there were two galleys and one brigantine.

When he saw such a multitude of ships, he acted like a most valiant captain: he called to him all his knights and men of the said ships, and then began to exhort and beseech them that, for the love of God and of the Christian faith, they would expose themselves willingly to suffer death, saying in this wise:

"O sirs, O brothers, now is the day that we must remember the Passion of Christ, and how much pain He endured to redeem us sinners. Now is that day when all our sins will be blotted out. For this I beseech you . . . to go vigorously against these dogs; for I hope that God will give us the victory. . . ."

And then the spiritual father stood upon the ship of the said captain, with the crucifix in his hand, and delivered a beautiful discourse to all. . . . And he knew so well how to speak, that the greater part of us wept, and prayed God that He would cause us to die in that battle.

In the meantime the immense fleet of the Moors came toward us to pass by. On that same day, our captain [Don Lourenço] departed with two ships and went toward the Moors, and passed between two ships, which were the largest in the Moorish fleet. And when he passed between the said ships, he saluted both of them with very great discharges of artillery; and this our captain did in order to know these two ships, and how they behaved. . . . Nothing more was done that day.

Early on the following morning [March 17, 1506], the Moors began all to make sail and come toward the city of Cananore, and sent to our captain to say that he should let them pass. . . . Our captain sent to them to say that the Moors of Calicut would not allow Christians to return who were staying in Calicut in their faith, but killed forty-eight of them, and robbed them of three thousand ducats between goods and money. And then he said to them:

"Pass, if pass you can, but first know what sort of people Christians are."

Said the Moors: "Our Mahomet will defend us from you Christians."

And so began all to sail with the greatest fury, wishing to pass, and they always navigate near the land, eight or ten miles. Our captain allowed them to come until they arrived opposite the city of Cananore . . . because the king of Cananore was looking on, and to show him how great was the courage of the Christians. And when it was the time for eating, the wind began to freshen a little, and our captain said:

"Now, up brothers, for now is the time; for we are all good knights"—and began to go toward these two largest ships.

It would be impossible to describe to you the kinds of instruments which they sounded, according to their custom. Our captain grappled valiantly with one of the ships of the Moors, that is, the largest, and three times the Moors threw off our grappling irons; at the fourth time we remained fast, and immediately our Christians leaped on board the said ship, in which there were six hundred Moors. Here, a most cruel battle was fought with immense effusion of blood, so that not one escaped from this ship: they were all killed.

Then our captain went to find the other very large ship of the Moors, which was now grappled fast by another of our ships; and here also a cruel battle was fought, in which five hundred Moors died. When

these two large ships were taken, all the rest of the fleet of the Moors fought with desperation, and divided our sixteen ships, so that there were some of our ships which had around them fifteen or twenty of those of the Moors to fight. . . .

Once our brigantine separated a little from the ships, and was immediately placed in the middle of four of the Moorish ships; and they fought her sharply, and at one time fifteen Moors were on the brigantine, so that the Christians had all withdrawn to the poop. When the valiant captain named Simon Martin saw that there were so many Moors upon the brigantine, he leaped amongst these dogs, and said: "O Jesus Christ, give us the victory! help thy faith!" and with the sword in his hand he cut off the heads of six or seven. All the other Moors threw themselves into the sea and fled, some here, some there.

When the other Moors saw that this brigantine had gained the victory, four other ships went to succor their people. The captain of the brigantine, seeing the said Moors coming, immediately took a barrel which had contained powder, and then he took a piece of a sail and thrust it in the bunghole of the said barrel, which appeared like the stone of a mortar, and he put a handful of powder over the barrel, and standing with fire in his hand, made as though he were going to fire a mortar.

The Moors, seeing this, thought that the said barrel was a mortar, and immediately turned back. And the said captain withdrew where the Christians were with his brigantine, victorious. . . .

When the Moors saw so many of their ships sunk, and that the two ships, the captains of the fleet and others were taken, they immediately took to flight, some one way, some another, some by land, some by sea, some in the port, some in the opposite direction. At the conclusion, our captain [Don Lourenço], seeing all our ships safe, said:

"Praised be Jesus Christ, let us follow up our victory against these dogs"—and so we all together set ourselves to follow them. . . .

And then they were pursued all night, so that all this fleet was put to flight without the death of a single Christian; and our ships which remained here followed another large ship, which was tacking out at sea. Finally our ships prevailed over theirs . . . so that all the Moors cast themselves into the sea to swim, and we constantly followed them to the shore in the skiff, with crossbows and lances killing and wounding them. . . .

On the following morning, our captain [Don Lourenço] sent the galleys, the brigantine, with some other vessels, along the shore, to see what bodies they could count. They found that those who were killed on the shore and at sea, and those of the ships taken, were counted at thirty-six hundred dead bodies. . . .

The king of Cananore, seeing all this battle, said: "These Christians are very brave and valiant men."

And truly I have found myself in some battles in my time, but I never saw any men more brave than these Portuguese.

The Battle of Diu

Don Lourenço's crushing defeat of the Calicut convoy fitted in with Almeida's plans to destroy Indian naval units before the Egyptian fleet arrived. That arrival was delayed by difficulties encountered in transporting wood to Suez to build the ships.

Early in 1508 Don Lourenço again took a task force north, scouting for the Egyptians. Off Chaul, in March, a lookout sighted sails on the horizon, but as the white specks became larger Don Lourenço saw that the rig was European and concluded the ships were Portuguese.

A veteran seaman on Don Lourenço's caravel began to put on his armor. Some younger hands laughed at him.

"I see no crosses on the sails of those ships," said the veteran grimly.

Too late, Don Lourenço and the Portuguese awoke to recognize the Red Sea fleet of the Sultan of Egypt, under the green banner of Mohammed, bearing down upon them.

Bravely, Don Lourenço led his eight caravels in a line toward the thirteen Egyptian ships and more than one hundred light Indian and Arabian vessels. But artillery, fired with chilling accuracy by the sultan's Venetian gunners, drove the Portuguese ships back, and they fled.

Only Don Lourenço, who had been court-martialed by his father at the end of 1507 for allowing some Indian vessels to evade him, stayed and fought. With one leg smashed by a cannon ball, the giant youth sat in a chair on deck and directed his men as they beat off four boarding parties. Then another shot killed Don Lourenço, and his ship was taken and sunk.

The news that the Portuguese had been routed at sea was electrifying. Their Indian allies began to desert them, and the stock market at Venice soared.

"He who has eaten the cockerel must eat the cock, or pay the price," muttered Almeida.

The viceroy was heartbroken over the loss of his only son; he blamed himself bitterly for the rebuke he had given Don Lourenço. He was now a changed man—harsh, cruel, obsessed with one idea: to win back the dominion of the seas and avenge his son's death.

Almeida stripped Portuguese garrisons in East Africa (Kilwa) and India (Cochin, Cananore) of men and arms. Clerks were snatched from their desks in factories, and had swords thrust into hands accustomed only to wielding long quill pens. Crossbows, swords, pikes, double-bladed axes, breastplates, and leather jerkins were at a premium.

On December 12, 1508, a war fleet of nineteen vessels bearing thirteen hundred Portuguese fighting men and four hundred picked Hindus slid silently from its anchorage at Cananore and headed north.

The Portuguese met the Red Sea fleet of Egypt, supported by small Indian vessels, on the morning of February 2, 1509, off the city of Diu. Almeida at once ordered his ships to take the position from which the wind was blowing. Portholes on the gundecks were opened, cannon wheeled forward (many of them with names like "The Butcher" or "The Lion"), and the Portuguese began a long-range bombardment.

At midday the enemy showed signs of disarray; the caravels came about and sailed down upon them. Almeida's ship grappled with one of the two largest Egyptian ships, while his lieutenant, Pereira, closed with the flagship of the Egyptian commander, Emir Hussein.

Portuguese boarding parties leaped the rails and crashed into mail-clad Mamelukes, the sultan's bodyguard. After a bloody five-hour battle, Emir Hussein dashed into a small boat and escaped. But above the jumble of bodies, from the masthead of the Egyptian flagship, flew the blue *quinas* of Portugal's flag.

The Indian-Egyptian fleet was scattered, sails in tatters, gaping holes in the hulls. Some ships escaped at nightfall, but most of the enemy vessels were either sunk or captured. And now, for thousands of miles, from China to the Cape of Good Hope, there was no naval force to challenge the smoke-blackened mariners of Portugal. Nor would there be for a hundred years.

The caravels had won an empire.

Epilogue

Diu was one of the decisive battles in history. If the embittered Almeida had lost, if the Moslems had kept their monopoly of the rich Indian commerce, Christian Europe might have remained economically dependent upon Islam. Still more of Europe's small supply of gold would have been drained off to the East to pay for spices and luxury goods. Exploration of the New World would have been handicapped by lack of funds. The Turks might have had the resources to capture Vienna early in the sixteenth century, then to press on through Austria and threaten France and England.

Instead, the Turks were driven back. The cities of Italy, for two hundred years the centers of Renaissance wealth and culture, saw their trade and wealth pass first to Lisbon and Seville, then to Antwerp and London in the north. Rembrandt, Rubens, Camoens, and Shakespeare came to the fore as Italian painting and poetry declined. The Medicis gave way, as patrons of art and literature, to Manuel of Portugal, Charles V of Spain, Francis I of France, and Elizabeth of England. Genoa and Venice ceased to be centers of world trade, although some spices were still shipped by way of Venice. The Renaissance moved from Italy to Germany and into western Europe.

Portuguese efforts to capture the spice trade also hastened the search for another sea route to the East, and thus the discovery and exploration of the New World. Envious of the success of the Portuguese in rounding Africa, Spain was willing to finance Columbus's four voyages to America, and later sent Magellan to the frozen wastes of Patagonia to seek a *southwest* passage to the spice islands of Asia. England dispatched Frobisher and Hudson to seek a *northwest* passage, Willoughby to look for a *northeast* passage. Holland's Barents and Linschoten also tried, without success, to sail through mountains of ice over the top of Siberia to Japan. In the middle of the sixteenth century Gomara proposed that Spain build a Panama Canal. All these countries—stimulated by Portugal's success—made settlements in the Americas.

Portugal and Spain founded Europe's first world empires, and—at the start—Portugal's was by far the more extensive and profitable. Almeida's successor, Albuquerque, greatest of viceroys, firmly based his country's holdings on three fortresses rimming the Indian Ocean: Ormuz, Goa, and Malacca. By 1600 these holdings had expanded to the Spice Islands and the coast of China. Elaborate churches and government buildings adorned the capital, "Golden Goa," where St. Francis Xavier, the famous missionary, rebuked merchants for their cruelty to slaves and walked the dusty streets ringing his bell to bring children and slaves out to him. Only when the Dutch found a new sailing route to Indonesia (voyaging due east from the Cape of Good Hope, then north) and when a chronic manpower shortage and bureaucratic corruption had taken their toll, did the Portuguese dominion decline.

For four hundred years after Almeida's victory other European nations—France, Holland, England, Belgium, Germany, Russia, and Italy—followed the example of

Portugal and Spain. The colonial system, which since World War II has been everywhere under attack, saw its beginnings in the voyages of da Gama, Cabral, and Almeida. The "old man of Belem," the prophetic figure whom Camoens invented for his epic poem celebrating da Gama's expedition, warned the Portuguese that in their quest for empire they were sowing the wind and would reap the whirlwind. Perhaps his words are better understood by twentieth century Europeans and Americans, who must live through the effects of today's revolutions in Asia and Africa.

For the great historical movement initiated by the Portuguese kings and captains is coming to an end. Never again, apparently, will an Albuquerque rule with an iron hand in "Portuguese Asia," nor even a heroic Western missionary like St. Francis Xavier be the representative of Christianity in India and Japan. Foreign businessmen and foreign religious leaders alike are being replaced. In the future, administrators, priests, and ministers will be natives of the lands in which they hold office, as new nations are born from the old colonial empires. The peoples of the earth are striving, today, to live together as equals.

But that West met East at all, and that they mingled as they have, is in large part due to the Portuguese pioneers of the Ocean Sea. For two centuries, inspired by a fervent, unquestioning faith and a taste for adventure and fortune, Portugal sent its young men, its lifeblood, abroad. Only one in ten came back. They carried Western ideas and inventions to the most remote places on the globe.

Any map tells their story. From the Cape of Good Hope to the Strait of Magellan, from Greenland to Formosa, there is scarcely a coast on which the countrymen of Prince Henry did not land a caravel, name a cape, plant a *padrão*, or build a fortress. In Brazil their language and their culture are spread through half a continent.

"God gave the Portuguese a small land for their birthplace," said a missionary, "but all the world to die in."

For better or for worse, Cão, Dias, and Vasco da Gama wakened Europe from the dreams and visions of a thousand years and showed it the wide world as they sailed their ships down the "Green Sea of Darkness," eastward to India.

Bibliography

Sources for the Portuguese Voyages

Azurara, Gomes Eannes de, *The Chronicle of the Discovery and Conquest of Guinea,* tr. and ed. Charles Raymond Beazley and Edgar Prestage. London, Hakluyt Society, 1896–99.

Berjeau, J. Ph., tr. and ed., *Calcoen: a Dutch Narrative of the Second Voyage of Vasco da Gama to Calicut.* London, B. M. Pickering, 1874.

Corrêa, Gaspar, *The Three Voyages of Vasco da Gama,* tr. and ed. Henry E. J. Stanley. London, Hakluyt Society, 1869.

Crone, G. R., tr. and ed., *The Voyages of Cadamosto.* London, Hakluyt Society, 1937.

Greenlee, William Brooks, tr. and ed., *The Voyage of Pedro Alvares Cabral to Brazil and India.* London, Hakluyt Society, 1938.

Ley, Charles David, ed., *Portuguese Voyages 1498–1663.* London, J. M. Dent and Sons, Ltd., 1947.

Ravenstein, E. G., ed., *A Journal of the First Voyage of Vasco da Gama, 1497–1499.* London, Hakluyt Society, 1898.

Later Books About the Portuguese Voyages

Beazley, C. Raymond, *Prince Henry the Navigator.* New York, G. P. Putnam's Sons, 1897.

Camões, Luiz de, *The Lusiads,* tr. and ed. Leonard Bacon. New York, Hispanic Society of America, 1950.

Danvers, Frederick C., *The Portuguese in India; Being a History of the Rise and Decline of Their Eastern Empire.* London, W. H. Allen and Company, Ltd., 1894.

Freitas, William, *Camoens and His Epic.* Stanford University, 1963.

Hart, Henry H., *Sea Road to the Indies.* New York, The Macmillan Company, 1950.

Herrmann, Paul, *The Great Age of Discovery.* New York, Harper and Brothers, 1958.

Jayne, Kingsley G., *Vasco da Gama and His Successors, 1460–1580.* London, Methuen and Company, Ltd., 1910.

Morison, Samuel Eliot, *Portuguese Voyages to America in the Fifteenth Century.* Cambridge, Harvard University Press, 1940.

Nowell, Charles E., *A History of Portugal.* New York, D. Van Nostrand Company, Inc., 1952.

Oliveira Martins, Joaquim Pedro de, *The Golden Age of Prince Henry the Navigator.* London, Chapman and Hall, Ltd., 1914.

Penrose, Boies, *Travel and Discovery in the Renaissance 1420–1620.* Cambridge, Harvard University Press, 1952.

Prestage, Edgar, *The Portuguese Pioneers.* London, A. & C. Black, Ltd., 1933.

Sanceau, Elaine, *Henry the Navigator.* New York, W. W. Norton and Company, Inc., 1947.

Whiteway, Richard S., *The Rise of Portuguese Power in India, 1497–1550.* Westminster, A. Constable and Company, 1899.

A Timetable of Events

1415   Prince Henry the Navigator takes part in the
        Portuguese capture of Ceuta, a Moorish strong-
        hold opposite Gibraltar.

1418   Tristão Vaz Teixeira and John Gonçalves Zarco
        set out for Guinea but accidentally rediscover
        the Madeira Islands.

1420   Teixeira and Zarco begin the colonization of
        the Madeiras; Perestrello's rabbits cause them
        trouble.

1425   A Portuguese expeditionary force explores the
        Canary Islands but fails to conquer the primitive
        inhabitants.

1432   Gonçalo Velho rediscovers the Azores, only
        1,054 miles from Newfoundland.

1434   Gil Eannes, encouraged by Prince Henry, sails
        past Cape Bojador, Morocco, the southern limit
        of the known world.

1441   Antão Gonçalves and Nuno Tristão bring back
        to Portugal the first African slaves taken by
        Europeans.

1448   Prince Henry has a fort built at Arguim, north of the Senegal River, where the Portuguese buy a thousand slaves a year from Arab traders, for resale in Portugal.

1456   Alvise da Cadamosto, blown west by a storm, discovers the arid Cape Verde Islands, three hundred miles from the African mainland.

1460   Prince Henry the Navigator dies, having sent his captains as far south as Guinea in the search for a sea road to India.

1473   Fernão Gomes sends his ships across the equator.

1482   King John II has a fortress built at Elmina ("The Mine") on the Guinea Gold Coast, giving Portugal control of the Guinea trade in gold, ivory, and slaves.

1482   Diogo Cão reaches the Congo River, where he plants a *padrão*.

1484   King John II and his committee of scholars reject Christopher Columbus's plan to reach Asia by a westward voyage.

1485   Diogo Cão sails one hundred miles up the Congo, then south to Cape Cross, less than eight hundred miles from the Cape of Good Hope.

1487   King John II sends Pero de Covilhan and

Afonso de Paiva overland to seek Prester John and information about a sea route to India.

1487–88   Bartholomew Dias doubles the Cape of Good Hope and enters the Indian Ocean.

1495   King John II dies and is succeeded by King Manuel the Fortunate.

1497–98   Vasco da Gama sails around the Cape of Good Hope to India and returns with samples of ivory, gold, gems, and spices.

1500–01   Pedro Alvares Cabral accidentally discovers Brazil; in Calicut, his men are attacked and he bombards the city.

1502   Vasco da Gama bombards Calicut, sinks Arab merchant vessels, and makes a trade treaty with Cochin.

1505   Francisco de Almeida establishes Portuguese bases in East Africa and on the west coast of India.

1506   Lourenço Almeida, with a task force of eleven ships, routs a fleet of 209 small Indian vessels.

1508   Lourenço Almeida's task force is surprised by the Egyptian Red Sea fleet of Emir Hussein; the Portuguese are defeated, and Lourenço is killed.

1509   Francisco de Almeida, with a force of nineteen ships, destroys Emir Hussein's Red Sea fleet at the Battle of Diu, giving Portugal control of the Indian Ocean.

Cast of Characters

PERO DE ALENQUER. Chief pilot for both Bartholomew Dias and Vasco da Gama. Confident, skillful; wears silk garments and gold neck chain.

FRANCISCO DE ALMEIDA. Gallant naval commander, first Viceroy of India, victor at the crucial battle of Diu.

LOURENÇO ALMEIDA. Son of Viceroy Almeida, an eighteen-year-old of giant physique, the best swordsman in Portugal.

GOMES EANNES DE AZURARA. Scholarly historian of Prince Henry's African voyages who greatly admires the prince but is moved to pity by the suffering of his African slaves.

PEDRO ALVARES CABRAL. Polished, idealistic young noble-man, commander of the second expedition to India.

ALVISE DA CADAMOSTO. Observant young Venetian sea captain who seeks his fortune on a voyage to Africa in the service of Prince Henry and writes a book about his experiences.

PEDRO VAZ DE CAMINHA. Member of Cabral's expedition and courtier in King Manuel's household who writes King Manuel an account of Cabral's landing in Brazil.

LUIS DE CAMOENS. Greatest of Portuguese poets, author of the epic about Vasco da Gama's voyage, *The Lusiads*; brave, adventurous, romantic.

DIOGO CÃO. A sea captain of common birth, descendant of a bailiff; the first European to reach the Congo River.

NICOLAS COELHO. Brave captain of the *Berrio*, the first ship in Vasco da Gama's fleet to return to Portugal from India.

CHRISTOPHER COLUMBUS. Tall, red-haired, blue-eyed Genoese who is convinced he can reach Asia by sailing west; boastful, talkative, devout, determined.

PERO DE COVILHAN. Skilled linguist and man of action who becomes a loyal intelligence agent for King John II in the East.

BARTHOLOMEW DIAS. Experienced captain and outstanding navigator who rounds the Cape of Good Hope in a storm and reaches the threshold of India.

DIOGO DIAS. A capable navigator, like his brother Bartholomew; the first European to reach Madagascar.

GIL EANNES. First captain to sail past Cape Bojador, Morocco, southern limit of the known world; timorous, then bold.

PAUL DA GAMA. A quiet, efficient captain who lacks Vasco's physical stamina; cheerful, considerate, takes good care of his seamen.

VASCO DA GAMA. Fearless captain-major of the first Portuguese expedition to reach India and one of the three greatest navigators of the Age of Discovery; suspicious, at times cruel. Devoted to his brother Paul.

FERNÃO GOMES. Profit-seeking Lisbon businessman who sends ships to explore fifteen hundred miles farther south along the African coast in return for a five-year monopoly of the Guinea trade.

ANTÃO GONÇALVES. Adventure-seeking young chamberlain of Prince Henry's household who captures the first African slaves taken by the Portuguese.

PRINCE HENRY THE NAVIGATOR. Crusader and scientist, strong-willed prince who sends out expedition after expedition to explore the African coast and seek a sea route to India.

EMIR HUSSEIN. Confident commander of the Egyptian Red Sea fleet which is defeated by Viceroy Almeida's Portuguese force off Diu.

KING JOHN II. A young ruler of great ability, who crushes opposition at home, then organizes expeditions which discover the way to India; warrior, administrator, and diplomat, the "Perfect Prince."

KING MANUEL THE FORTUNATE. A cold, calculating ruler who profits by King John II's labors; excellent administrator but often ungrateful to commanders who serve under him.

MONÇAIDE. Outspoken Moor from North Africa who greets Vasco da Gama's men when they arrive in Calicut and later warns them of a Moslem plot.

DUARTE PACHECO PEREIRA. Skilled navigator, writer, and military commander who defends Portuguese fort at Cochin against overwhelming numbers, writes an important treatise on navigation.

JOHN DA SÁ. Vasco da Gama's clerk, who is skeptical of the "Christianity" of Calicut; later, commands the *St. Gabriel.*

TRISTÃO VAZ TEIXEIRA and JOHN GONÇALVES ZARCO. Young squires of Prince Henry's household who ask Prince Henry for an opportunity to win fame and by chance rediscover the Madeira Islands.

LUDOVICO DI VARTHEMA. Italian adventurer who fights with the Portuguese against the Indian fleet of the Zamorin, and writes an account of the battle.

GONÇALO VELHO. Commander in the Order of the Knights of Christ who captains expedition which rediscovers the Azores.

ZAMORIN OF CALICUT. Bland, cunning Indian ruler who wishes to please both the Portuguese and the established Arab traders but underestimates Vasco da Gama.

Index